The two masted schooner *Pythian* out of Gloucester, Massachusetts went ashore and was sunk at Kittery Point in a gale on February 1, 1908. The crew of thirteen were all saved but the vessel was badly damaged. Salvagers floated her a month later and she was towed to Gloucester. She was converted to a motor vessel after her accident. *Photo courtesy of Brewster Harding, Portland, Maine.*

SHIPWRECKS AROUND MAINE

(Illustrated)

By William P. Quinn

A collection of photographs and stories from the 1880's to the 1980's
of marine disasters along the coasts of Maine and New Hampshire.

Drawings by Paul C. Morris, Nantucket, Massachusetts.

The Revenue Service cutter *Manning* effecting a rescue at sea. The *Manning* was built in 1897 at the Atlantic Works in East Boston at a cost of $159,951. She performed rescue work along the New England and Pacific coastlines and also served with the Bering Sea Patrol Fleet. After 33 years of service she was retired and sold out of the service.

Library of Congress Catalog Card No. 83-80403
ISBN 0-936972-11-4

Printed in the United States of America by

> Bookcrafters, Incorporated
> Chelsea, Michigan

Published by

> The Lower Cape Publishing Co.
> P.O. Box 901, Orleans, Mass. 02653

FIRST EDITION

Other books by
William P. Quinn

SHIPWRECKS AROUND CAPE COD (1973)
SHIPWRECKS AROUND NEW ENGLAND (1978)

PREFACE

This book is a collection of photographs of marine accidents along the Maine coast covering the period from the early 1880's to the early 1980's. Some were copied from old prints loaned by friends. A few of the photos have been published before but are included as part of the collection. Not all of the shipwrecks are listed as the number is far too great for the space available. The state of Maine has a long and unique maritime history. The early economy centered around marine commerce here and abroad. Shipwrecks were a common everyday occurrence along the coast. The graphic illustrations will locate the reader at the scene of the wreck; the captions and text will recount the details of the incident. Information has been gleaned from newspapers, magazines, Government reports and interviews with witnesses. The early Life Saving Service and later the Coast Guard were the saviors in many cases of wreck and disaster. Thousands of persons and millions in property have been saved by these marine vanguards. The accidents range along the entire coastline of Maine and New Hampshire. Some are at far away places, involving Maine ships and other ships with the name of Maine. The state has many coastal scenic treasures. Some of the lighthouses are depicted to show the reader the overwhelming beauty of this spectacular land. Over the past one hundred years, ship accidents were common occurrences but today, modern technology has reduced the disasters to rare incidents. Man however, cannot control the weather which is the primary cause of shipwrecks.

This book is dedicated to my two sons:
William Jr. and Leslie

    The tugboats *Express* and *Willard Clapp* sunk at Saco, sometime around the turn of the century. This is a fascinating photograph which careful study will reveal much about marine salvage operations of the period. In the background is a salvage lighter. On deck, a diver is sitting on the railing, his helmet is at his side. The air pump is to his left and it appears that he is getting ready to dive on the sunken tugs. The *Express* was the larger of the two vessels. She might have sprung a leak and sank, taking the smaller tug *Willard Clapp* down with her as the two vessels were probably tied to each other. The salvage effort is being viewed by a large crowd of men on the right, most of whom have derby hats which dates the photograph near the 1900 period. *Photo courtesy of Steven Lang, Owls Head, Maine.*

CONTENTS

CHAPTER

1 The early years. Maine's Rocky coast. Bailey's Mistake, shipwreck evidence etched in stone and the establishment of the Life Saving Service. 1

2 Maine's shipbuilding industry. The development of Photography. The *City of Richmond,* the *Katahdin* and the Dead Ship of Harpswell 13

3 Maine's maritime commerce; lumber, lime and ice. The Revenue Cutter *Woodbury,* Remember the *Maine* and the Portland Gale of 1898 19

4 A new era with automobiles and wireless communications for ships. The *Washington B. Thomas,* the *Fannie & Edith,* Whale Back Rock and the *Lizzie Carr* 31

5 The Down-Easters, the Giant Schooners and the Steamers of Maine. The famous collision. Unconventional Launchings and the decline of the coastal schooner 47

6 The *Titanic* and the *Empress of Ireland.* World War I and the *Kronprinzessin Cecilie,* the *Bay State* and the loss of the *Alma E.A. Holmes* 63

7 The Ghost Schooner of Maine. Cape Porpoise and the *Trickey.* The Rum Runners, Trundy's Reef and the wreck of the *City of Rockland* 83

8 The decline of the Maine Passenger Steamers. The grounding of the *Iroquois* and the *Sagamore.* Rum Running ends and the tragic loss of the *Squalus* 103

9 World War II and the loss of the *Don.* The tale of the *U.S.S. Buchanan.* German Spies, radar and helicopters. The wreck of the *Oakey L. Alexander* 113

10 The Coast Guard today along the Maine coast; modern equipment speeds rescues with helicopters, planes and modern vessels. Operations, and the lighthouses of Maine 127

11 The space age arrives with computers and satellites. The wrecks continue with the loss of the *Bear* and the *Ambassador.* The *Musashino Maru* aground in Searsport 139

12 The Blizzard of 1978. Some yacht wrecks. The Falkland Islands wrecks and the marijuana smugglers. The *John F. Leavitt* and two Monhegan silver medals 159

LIST OF PHOTOGRAPHS

Abbie Burgess grave 8
Albatross HU-16E 132
Alice E. Clark 46
Alma E.A. Holmes 71
Alton A. 148, 149
Ambassador 142
Amphialos 144
Andarte 140
Anne C. Maguire 16
Annie L. Henderson 43
Annie Mary 107
Armeria 23
Arthur Seitz 53
Athenian Star 153

Bailey's Mistake 4
Bath Iron Works 176
Bay State 76, 77
Bear 141
Berwindvale 106
Bessie Parker 43
Biscayne Freeze 137
Bluenose 175
Bohemian 6
Boothbay 45
Boothbay Harbor Schooners 56
Bouchard Barge B No. 105 160
Brandon 98
Bull Moose 167

Cambridge 15
Camilla May Page 99
Carroll A. Deering 82
Casco Bay hulks 107
Cape Elizabeth Life Saving Station 128
Cape Elizabeth Lighthouse 134
Charles H. Trickey 82
Christian F. Reinauer 165
Cimbria 24
City of Bangor 34, 35
City of New York 126
City of Richmond 12
City of Rockland 42, 90, 91
Coast Guard Base, South Portland 129
Coast Guard Cutter Duane 136
Coast Guard 41' boat 128
Coast Guard Helicopters 130, 131
Cora F. Cressy 59
Courtney C. Houck 118
Cowslip 121
Cresta 125

David Cohen 54
Diving Bell 109
Diving to Submarine Squalus 109
Dorothy 101
D.T. Sheridan 122, 123

Edna M. McKnight 56
Eleanor A. Percy 51
Eleazer Boynton 65
Elizabeth Howard 79
Ellen M. Mitchell 44
Emily F. Northam 96, 97
Empire Knight 117
Empire Thrush 116
Empress 20
Empress of Ireland 69
Erie 21
Eva May 29
Express VI

Falcon 108
Fannie and Edith 30

Fannie & Fay 65
Federal Monarch 143
First Light House District 10
F.J. Lisman 69
Flying Lifeboat, HH-52A 130

Gardner G. Deering 52
General R.N. Batchelder 100
George W. Wells 50, 51
Goose Rocks Lighthouse 135
Gov. Bodwell 92
Governor Robie 16
Guardian HU-25A Jet 132

Hattie Eaton Marker 11
Helen B. Crosby 44
Helen J. Seitz 54
Henry B. Hyde 37
Henry L. Peckham 55
Herman F. Kimball 81
Herman Winter 75
Hesper 60
Hockomock 101
Howard W. Middleton 49
Hungarian 6
Hunniwells Beach Lifeboat 32

Ice House fires 55
Indomable 169
Iroquois 104

Jennifer 152
Jewel Island 7
John F. Leavitt 162, 163
John Neptune 173
Joseph Luther 33
Joseph P. Connelly 122
J.T. Morse 62, 74, 93

Katahdin 14
Katie J. Barrett 22
Keating 48
Kickapoo 106
Kings County 105
Kronprinzessin Cecilie 70

Lannie Cobb 74
Little Mark Island 11
Lizzie Carr 40, 41
Lochinvar 102
Luther Little 60

Maine (Battleship) 25
Maine (Tanker) 115
Manhattan 62
Manning IV
Marine Merchant 140
Marshall Point Lighthouse 138
Mary Ann 145
Mary A. Brown 36
Mary Bradford Peirce 58
Mary E. Olys 82
Mary H. Diebold 57
Mary Langdon 94
Mary Weaver 57
Massasoit 45
Matinicus Rock Lighthouse 9
Mattie 146
Maude M. Morey 61
Maureen & Michael 144
Miss Faye III 155
Monhegan 105
Musashino Maru 156, 157

Northern Gulf 141
Northern Miner 159
Norumbega 68, 70
Nubble Lighthouse X

Oakey L. Alexander 119, 120, 121
Onalay 161
Ortem 168
Ossipee 87

Pemaquid 113
Pemaquid Point Lighthouse 135
Penobscot 36
Pilgrim 100
Polias 86
Portland 26, 27, 28
Portland Head Lighthouse .134
Portland Lightship 129, 179
Portland Observatory 11
Pythian II

Queen Elizabeth II 176

Rachael Ann 172
Ransom B. Fuller 41, 85
Reine Marie Stewart 181
Robert W. 87
Royal Tar 2
Rum Runner 95

Sabino 80
Sadie and Lillie 37
Sagamore 104
Scotia Prince 175
Seaward 84, 85
Seguin 112, 151
Seguin Lighthouse 10
Shamrock 95
Shenendoah 47
Sikorsky HH-3F Helicopter 131
Silver Medals 166

Snohomish 133
Snow Squall 171
Sophia 79
Spindrift 48
Squalus Recovery 110, 111
Squalus Conning Tower 111
St. Christopher 124
St. Mary 170
St. Nicholas 150
St. Patrick 149

Tamano 147
Tay 64
Thalassa 145
Titanic 66
Torpedoed Survivors 117
Tourist 80
Truro Queen 92
U.S.S. Duane 136, 137

Vernon Langille 167
Vinal Haven 103
Vincent Tibbets 158

Walborg 164
Wanby 88, 89
Washington B. Thomas 38, 39
Wawenock 99
West Quoddy Head Lighthouse 135
White Head Life Saving Station 73
Willard Clapp VI
William Booth 98
William L. Elkins 75
William P. Frye 72
William Rice 67
Willis & Guy 78
Wyoming 59

Young Brothers 55

Zebedee E. Cliff 61

Maine's marine heritage is displayed throughout the state. An example is this sign on Route 1 at the entrance to the historic shipbuilding town of Thomaston. *Photo by William P. Quinn.*

Above: The rocky coastline is prominent at Pemaquid Light, south of Damariscotta. Ocean waves are spectacular here during a storm. **Below:** Rocks are evident everywhere along the Maine Coast. This is Cape Neddick Light, more commonly called Nubble Light. A small island off the coast of York, it is a favorite of artists and photographers because of its beauty. *Photos by William P. Quinn.*

CHAPTER ONE

Around the world there are many dangerous coastlines. On our eastern seaboard, Cape Hatteras, Cape Cod and Sable Island are often called the graveyards of ships. Of all the hazardous navigation areas, the Maine coastline has proved notoriously treacherous for mariners since time immemorial. A shipwreck near the shore has fascinated those who witnessed it.

When the last glacier receded, the coast of Maine was formed. A seagull flying from Kittery to Calais would cover a distance of 228 miles. However, the glacier carved the coastline into 3,500 miles of shoreline with deep water inlets and large picturesque bays while forming over 2,000 islands. When the settlements were built, the water environment naturally led to the development of maritime commerce. In 1635, the first shipyard was established on Richmond Island, just south of Cape Elizabeth. Shipbuilding in Maine has flourished ever since. In the 300 or so years since ship construction began, countless vessels have met with accidents of one kind or another. Storms, groundings, collisions, fires, icebergs, sabotage, mutiny and drunken crewmen are just a few of the many causes of ships wrecked along the rocky coast of Maine.

The early mariners had no maps or books to guide them. Perhaps the first mishap that occurred was to the French explorer Samuel de Champlain. He ran aground on Mount Desert Island in 1604. Navigation along the coast was hazardous. Besides the fog banks, there were the concealed ledges and rocks. There were no buoys, lighthouses or other aids to navigation. One of Maine's tragic shipwrecks was the *Nottingham Galley* on December 11, 1710. The vessel was smashed ashore on Boon Island, a desolate piece of rock. There was no food or water to sustain the stranded crewmen. The ordeal lasted for 25 days before a rescue boat arrived from the mainland, but in that time the men had resorted to cannibalism to keep from starving.

There were many other difficulties along the Maine coastline. Congressional appropriations for light houses and other aids were slow in coming. An example was Halfway Rock. This small rock islet is about in the middle of the southern part of Casco Bay. Rocky ledges extend out 1,000 feet southwestward and northward from its center. In June of 1835, the brig *Samuel* was wrecked on Halfway Rock with the loss of two men. Repeated requests for funds for the structure fell on deaf ears in Washington. The lighthouse was finally completed in 1871.

Not all shipwrecks were accidents. There is a legend about the notorious Captain Keiff who used to roam around Cliff Island in Casco Bay. During a stormy night, he would tie a lantern on his horse and show a false light to ships passing by. Captain Keiff would lure the vessels ashore, kill the crew and salvage the cargo. He is said to have buried the crewmen in a pasture on the island which today is know as Keiff's Garden.

Prior to 1874, when a ship was wrecked on the coast of Maine, the rescue of the crew was carried out by volunteers from shore when conditions permitted. At sea, the Revenue Cutter Service aided vessels in distress. There was no established rescue service along the shore to assist shipwrecked mariners. In 1873, Congress appropriated the necessary funds to build and man five Life Saving Stations along the Maine coast. The stations were built at West Quoddy Head, Cross Island, Browney's Island, Whitehead Island and Biddeford Pool. A sixth station in the district was built at Rye Beach, New Hampshire. In the beginning the stations were only manned for six months each year from November 1st to April 30th. The stations were equipped with mortars, breeches buoy gear, lifeboats and other necessary apparatus to carry out the work of rescue. During the wreck season of 1875-76, the Maine Lifesavers went to the aid of 18 vessels in peril. Assistance by the Life Savers saved all but one of the vessels.

Above: On October 25, 1836, while bound from St. John, N.B. to Portland, Maine the steamship *Royal Tar* burned and then sank in Penobscot Bay. The steamer had a circus with wild animals, a brass band and other passengers on board. The fire started because of an overheated boiler. There was smoke and flames; the passengers panicked and some went overboard and drowned. The Revenue Cutter *Veto* was nearby at North Haven and went to rescue as many persons as possible. Of almost 100 people on board, 32 were lost in the tragedy. All of the animals died in the fire and subsequent loss of the vessel. The burned hulk sank off Vinalhaven Island. *Photo courtesy of the Peabody Museum of Salem.* **Below:** A tragic wreck occurred at Cape Neddick on November 30, 1842. The barque *Isidore* was wrecked in a storm with the loss of all hands. The gravestone of Captain Leander Foss, age 36, is but one of many similar ones in the cemeteries all along the Maine Coast. *Photo by William P. Quinn.*

The 1876 annual report of the U.S. Life Saving Service contains an excellent description of the Maine coastline as a warning to mariners: "The coast of Maine is jagged and indented by glacial valleys of great variety of depth, forming numerous sounds, narrow bays and channels. The channels reach far out into the sea, and the uneven, rocky ridges between which they lie also extend far seaward, forming narrow capes, reefs, headlands, points and small islands. These channels and ridges usually extend in direction nearly north and south, but frequently those are found which cut across, more or less diagonally, the general course. This feature adds to the otherwise dangerous character of this coast, causing sharp peaks, submerged rocks, and peculiarly irregular soundings. All of these characteristics of this portion of the coast involve danger to the mariner; but on the other hand, they also afford him numerous excellent harbors of refuge and sheltering lees in the tempestuous weather so prevalent in this latitude."

It has been over 100 years since the Life Saving Service began its duty along the coastline of the United States. Since its inception over 200,000 lives and over two billion dollars in property have been saved by the Revenue Cutters and the men of the Life Saving Service. In 1915, the two organizations merged to become the United States Coast Guard and have since then proudly carried on the traditions of their predecessors. The old Life Savers used to say — "The rule book says you've got to go out, it doesn't say anything about coming back!" Most of them did come back; however not all were successful in their rescue efforts but no one ever shirked his duty.

The establishment of the Life Saving Service ameliorated the plight of the shipwrecked mariner but only on those months the men were on duty at the stations. On May 5, 1878, the ship *John Clark* was wrecked off Machiasport at 10 p.m., in a heavy southeast gale with rough seas and fog. The ship was of 1,079 tons, from Sandy Hook, New Jersey for Calais, Maine with a crew of twenty men. The ship struck a reef a short distance from shore and driving over it, went on the rocks where she quickly broke up. Most of the crew were left drifting on pieces of wreckage and two of them were drowned. The remainder managed to make it to a rock where they waited until the tide dropped and then waded ashore. The men walked a mile to get help at Cutler Harbor. The Life Saving Station had been closed for the summer just four days before the wreck.

A sailing ship wreck on Monhegan Island from an old post card.

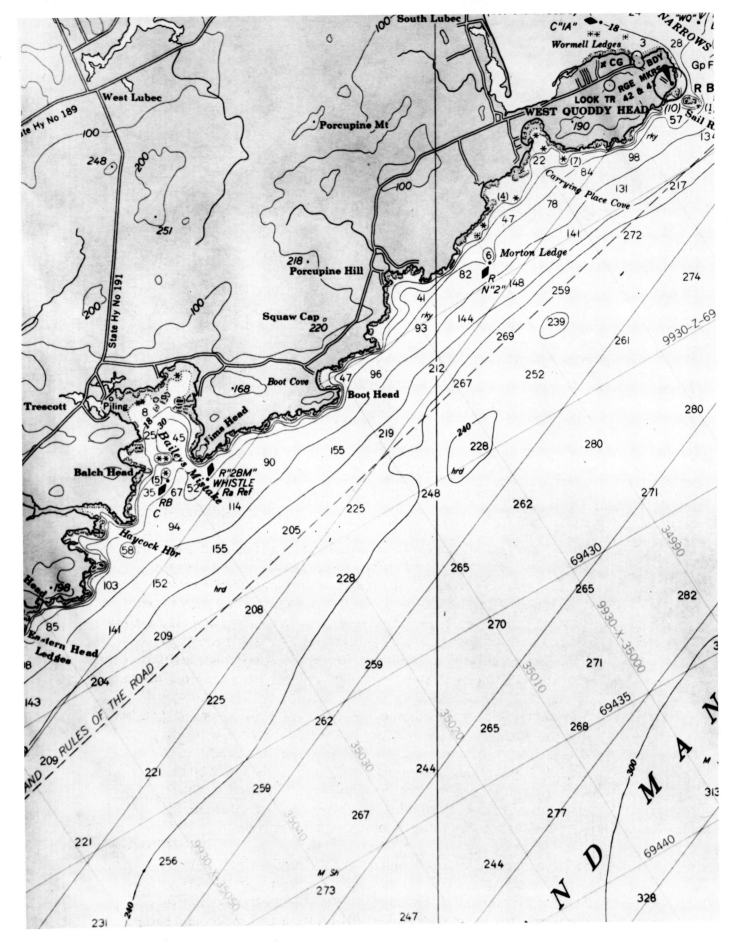

One of the more entertaining stories down Maine comes from Lubec about a shipwreck back in the early 1800's. It seems that a four masted schooner was battling a storm and fog off the coast at night and Capt. Bailey navigated his ship into what he thought was Quoddy Narrows. It turned out that he had made an error and went ashore near Trescott, seven miles west of the entrance to the narrows. The next morning, they found themselves high and dry. They were so embarrassed by such poor navigation, so the story goes, that they abandoned the schooner and settled right there on dry land. There is one flaw in the story however and that is the four masted schooner. The first one wasn't built in Maine until 1880. However, the mile wide bay became known as Bailey's Mistake and the U.S. Department of Commerce has bowed to local folklore and has marked the navigation charts and the Coast and Geodetic maps. The small bay at Trescott, Maine is marked plainly: Bailey's Mistake!

TALE OF THE KENNEBEC MARINER
By Holman F. Day

From: UP IN MAINE—Stories of Yankee Life told in verse.

Guess I' never told you, sonny, of the strandin' and the wreck
Of the steamboat *Ezry Johnson* that run up the Kennebec
That was 'fore the time of steam-cars, and the *Johnson* filled the bill
On the route between Augusty and the town of Waterville.

She was built old-fashioned model, with a bottom's flat's your palm
With a paddle-wheel behind her, driv' by one great churnin' arm
Couldn't say that she was speedy - sploshed along and made a touse
But she couldn't go much faster than a man could tow a house.
Still, she skipped and skived tremendous, dodged the rocks and skun the shoals,
In a way the boats of these days couldn't do to save their souls.
Didn't draw no 'mount of water, went on top instead of through.
This is how there come to happen what I'm going to tell to you.
-Hain't no need to keep you guessing, for I know you won't suspect
How that thunderin' old *Ez Johnson* ever happened to get wrecked.

She was overdue one ev'nin', fog come down most awful thick;
'Twas about like navigating round inside a feather tick
Proper caper was to anchor, but she seemed to run all right,
And we humped her - through 'twas resky - kept her sloshing through the night.

Things went on all right till morning, but along 'bout half-past three
Ship went dizzy, blind, and crazy - waves seemed wust I ever see.
Up she went and down she scuttered; sometimes seemed to stand on end,
Then she'd wallopse, sideways, crossways, in a way, by gosh to send
Shivvers down your spine. She'd teeter, fetch a spring, and take a bounce,
Then squat down, sir, on her haunches with a most je-roosly jounce,
Folks got up and run a-screaming, forced the wheelhouse, grabbed at me,
-Thought we'd missed Augusty landin' and had gone plum out to sea.
-Fairly shot me full of questions, but I said 'twas jest a blow;
Still that didn't seem to soothe 'em, for there warn't no wind, you know!
Yas, sir, spite of all that churnin', warn't a whisper of a breeze
-No excuse for all that upset and those strange and dretful seas.
Couldn't spy a thing around us - every way 'twas pitchy black,
And I couldn't seem to comfort them poor critters on my back.
Couldn't give 'em information, for 'twas dark's a cellar shelf;
-Couldn't tell 'em nothing 'about it - for I didn't know myself.

So I gripped the *Johnson's* tiller, kept the rudder riggin taut,
Kept a-praying, chawed tobacker, give her steam, and let her swat.
Now, my friend, jest listen stiddy: when the sun come out at four,
We warn't tossin' in the breakers off no stern and rockbound shore;
But I'd missed the gol-durned river, and I swow this 'ere is true,
There I was clear up in Sidney, and the tossings and the rolls
Simply happened 'cause we tackled sev'ral miles of cradle knolls.
Sun come out and dried the dew up; there she was a stranded wreck,
And they soaked me eighteen dollars' cartage to the Kennebec.

Above: The steamer *Bohemian* with 218 passengers and a crew of 99 was wrecked near Cape Elizabeth on February 22, 1864 in thick fog. It was early evening and the steamer was overdue from Liverpool. While entering Portland, she struck on Alden's Rock and stove a hole in her hull. Her Captain headed the vessel towards shore and she sunk on Broad Cove rocks. The lifeboats were launched to transfer the passengers to shore. One lifeboat swamped during launching and 42 persons were lost. The ship went to pieces on the rocks. *Photo courtesy of the Maine Historical Society, Portland.* **Below:** The *Hungarian,* a sistership to the *Bohemian,* a three deck bark rigged steamship. *From the Collection of Roger Peterson, Cape Elizabeth, Maine.*

Above: Jewel Island is the outermost island in Casco Bay. It was named after George Jewel who bought it from the Indians in 1637. There are many legends about Jewel Island. The most popular is that Captain Kidd's pirate treasure is buried there, somewhere on the island. Treasure hunters have dug many holes all over the island but so far, none of the booty has ever been found. Records indicate that the buccaneer never came anywhere near the island. Kidd's ghost is said to haunt the island whenever treasure hunters come ashore to search for his gold. During World War II, the United States Army came ashore and set up a base here. They installed seventy foot high watch towers along with coastal guns with everything connected by underground tunnels and bunkers. **Right:** The watch towers are still standing, looking out over the broad Atlantic Ocean. *Aerial photos by William P. Quinn.*

7

There have been many heroic lighthouse keepers but none more devoted to duty than Abbie Burgess, the heroine of Matinicus Rock. Abbie was only 17 when her father had to go ashore for food and supplies. He left the young girl to keep the light burning and to tend to her invalid mother and younger sisters. Winter storms prevented Samuel Burgess from returning to the rock for four weeks. During that time, Abbie worked day and night to care for her charges and she kept the light burning. This was in January, 1856, and Abbie repeated the effort again the following year when her father was gone for three weeks. Abbie later married Issac H. Grant and he subsequently became the keeper of the light. They raised four children on the rock. Abbie died in 1892 and is buried in Sprucehead. At the foot of her grave is a replica of the Matinicus Rock Lighthouse—Abbie is still keeper of the light.

Above: At a secluded cemetery in Sprucehead, Maine is the grave of Abbie E. Grant, the heroine of Matinicus Rock. **Below:** At the foot of her grave stands a replica of the Matinicus Rock Lighthouse. *Photos by William P. Quinn.*

Matinicus Rock is the southern most islet in the approach to Penobscot Bay, and is located about 30 miles from the mainland. The highest point on the island is only about 40 feet above sea level. Near the southern end of the island is the lighthouse, a 48 foot granite tower connected to a house with granite walls. In the foreground is the helicopter landing pad. *Photo courtesy of the U.S. Coast Guard, Boston, Mass.*

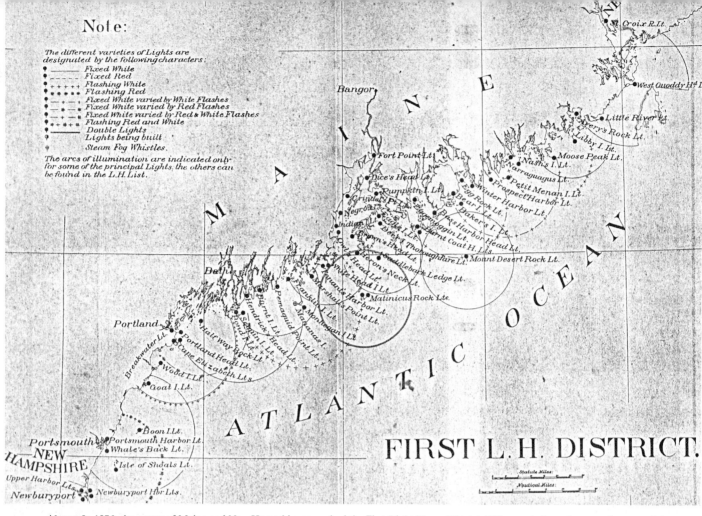

Above: In 1876, the coasts of Maine and New Hampshire comprised the First Light House District. This map is from the annual report of the Light House Board in Washington, D.C. It marks the fifty-five lighthouses along the district from the St. Croix River to the Isles of Shoals. The Lighthouse service dates back to colonial days in America. In the 19th century, in addition to lighthouses, the service maintained the aids to navigation and manned the lightships along the coast. **Below:** The Seguin Island Lighthouse was established in 1795 and rebuilt in 1857. The light tower is 180 feet above sea level. It is a 53-foot cylindrical tower connected to a dwelling and is at the summit of Seguin Island. There is a fog signal at the light. The lighthouse is one of the beauty spots in Maine. *Photo by James E. Perkins, courtesy of Jane Stevens, Bath, Maine.*

Above left: The Portland Observatory, built in 1807, is the last remaining 19th century signal tower standing on the Atlantic Coast. Situated on Munjoy Hill, it was used to signal townspeople upon the arrival of ships. The tower is open daily during the summer and offers a superb view of Casco Bay. **Above right:** In a small cemetery across the street from the Congregational Church at Kittery Point a unique gravestone tells of a fatal shipwreck that occurred on March 21, 1876. A picture of the wreck is carved in relief on the upper part of the stone. The brig *Hattie Eaton* was dashed on the rocks in a gale at Gerrish Island. In spite of efforts of townspeople on the beach, only one man was saved out of the nine on board. *Photos by William P. Quinn.* **Below:** Little Mark Island is located on the west side of Merriconeag Sound in the northern end of Casco Bay. The monument there was built in 1827 in the center of the island. It is a fifty foot high pyramidal tower painted white with a black stripe. There is a beacon on top and a room, twenty feet square at its base. This refuge for shipwrecked sailors is little more than a shelter designed to keep one dry during a summer rainstorm. *Aerial Photograph by William P. Quinn, Plane piloted by Hank Dempsey.*

11

Above: The *City of Richmond* was one of the fastest vessels in Maine waters. She ran from Portland to Rockland to Bar Harbor. On the morning of August 30, 1881 she ran up on the south ledge of Mark Island in the fog and then sank by the stern. The passengers, baggage and freight were loaded on other steamers and brought ashore safely. *Photo courtesy of the Penobscot Marine Museum, Searsport, Maine.* **Below:** The *City of Richmond* was raised from Mark Island and brought into Rockland and beached near Commercial Wharf. Later the vessel was towed to Portland and rebuilt. She was later sold and her name changed to the *City of Key West. Photo from the Marine Collection of Frank E. Claes.*

12

CHAPTER TWO

The first illustrations of shipwrecks were drawings by artists who tended to embellish slightly to fit the entire action into one picture. The art of photography was not perfected until after 1850. The French scientist Daguerre made reproductions on metal plates in 1839 and called them daguerrotypes. In time, new ideas in the field improved Daguerre's work but it wasn't until 1870 that faster plates were produced to make instant pictures possible. The later artists began to photograph shipwrecks and spectacular scenes were made of the disasters. By 1890, George Eastman had introduced roll film and the snapshot became a household pastime.

The state of Maine has a long and enviable record of shipbuilding. Maine built ships have sailed the oceans of the world since the middle of the 18th century. Clipper ships raced around Cape Horn for record passages. The clippers were followed by the Down-Easters. These beautiful vessels were rated high with ship-masters. Howard I. Chapelle in his "History of American Sailing Ships" said: "The part of the Maine shipbuilders and designers in the history of American Sailing Ships has never received full recognition. The so-called Down-Easters that followed the clippers were almost wholly the work of these men. Some of these vessels were, without a doubt, the highest development of a sailing ship; combining speed, handiness, cargo-capacity and low operating costs to a degree never obtained in any earlier square rigger." The next development in Maine shipbuilding was the great coal schooners. The fore-and-aft rigged vessels of 4, 5 and 6 masts were rated as the most economical cargo carriers ever built and were classed as prodigious money makers by their owners. The primary purpose of these vessels was the coal trade along the east coast. The schooners depended on the wind for quick passage. Many were lost in the frequent storms that lashed the coast in the winter. At other times, the insidious fog that rolls in along the Maine coast would blind the mariner and pile his ship on the rocks. The big schooner era had a life span of about fifty years as the steamships, operating on schedules, retired the schooners to the graveyard of ships.

For over 100 years, passenger travel by steamboat was popular along the Maine coast. Getting from one place to another was quick and easy compared to going overland for long distances on bad roads. In the beginning some of the wrecks were intentional when rival boats on the same routes would ram into each other to cut down on the competition. The business of passenger steamboats prospered in the second half of the 19th century all along the east coast. In Maine, a myriad of steamer lines operated from the interior to the coastal ports to connect with larger boats for Boston and the Maritimes. Accidents, while common, were usually minor, involving little or no loss of life. The companies made money until the 1930's when automobile and truck travel along paved roads ended the Maine steamboat era. Today, only the ferries operate to islands in Casco and Penobscot Bays. All of the Maine ferries are diesel powered. There are no more steamboats.

Above: The steamer *Katahdin* following her close call on the night of January 9, 1886 when she battled a gale off Cape Porpoise for 10 hours and won. *Photo from the marine collection of Frank E. Claes, Orland, Maine.* **Below:** The smashed wooden bulwarks of the steamer *Katahdin* are grim evidence of the terrible beating she took in the gale. Her heroic crew lined the sides of the vessel the next day beside the wharf at Portsmouth, New Hampshire. *Photo courtesy of the Steamship Historical Society of America.*

The *Katahdin* was a rugged side-wheel steamer of 1,234 tons, 241 feet long with a beam of 35 feet. She steamed in Maine waters, to and from Boston, for 30 years from 1863 until 1893 when she was retired. One night in her career stands out and will ever be remembered in the annals of steamboating.

It was 5:30 p.m., on January 8, 1866, when the steamer left Rockland for Boston under cloudy skies with 35 passengers and a large cargo. Later in the evening the wind rose and the seas became rough. Captain F.C. Homer had been through heavy seas before with the *Katahdin* and he wasn't concerned. By midnight however, the storm had increased to gale force with snow and high seas. The turbulent waters sent icy spray up over the ship where it quickly froze on decks and masts. At 1 a.m., the seas began to smash at the vessel carrying away wooden bulwarks and allowing the sea to board her. The deck cargo was swept overboard. Water began to cascade down into the coal bunkers. The vessel iced up badly and in the early morning, crewmen found the bunkers full of water.

Captain Homer knew if they lost steam, the vessel was doomed. The crew grabbed anything that would burn and fed it into the boilers. Benches, cabin doors, fittings, furniture and a large cargo of wooden spools all went into the fire to keep the steamer going. As the ship neared Boon Island, Captain Homer decided to turn towards shore hoping to make it into Portsmouth Harbor. After a ten hour battle with the sea, the *Katahdin* limped into the harbor with just enough steam to reach the wharf. She had eight feet of water in her hold. There was much praise for the Captain and crew for saving the ship and her passengers. After some repairs were made, the steamer loaded coal and left for Boston for an overhaul and refitting.

The steamer *Cambridge* was built in 1867 and was popular on the Boston-Bangor run. Her mysterious grounding on Old Man's Ledge off Port Clyde has never been explained. She was wrecked on February 10, 1886, on a clear moonlit night. All of her passengers and crew were rescued. The vessel was hung on the ledge amidships and when the tide went down she split in two. That night, heavy seas washed her off the ledge and the two halves sank. The ship was a total loss. *Drawing by Paul C. Morris, Nantucket, Massachusetts.*

Above: The bark *Anne C. Maguire* was driven up on the ledges, 100 yards from the Portland Head Lighthouse on Christmas Eve, Dec. 1886. The vessel hit so hard she shook the lighthouse. The crew was saved by breeches-buoy but the ship was a total loss. *Photo from the marine collection of Frank E. Claes, Orland, Maine.* **Below:** On March 5, 1889 at 2 a.m. in thick fog the ship *Governor Robie* of Bath came ashore at Fortunes Rocks near Kennebunkport. Life Savers from the Fletcher's Neck station launched a boat and proceeded to the scene of the wreck. When they arrived they ran hawsers to tugs but as the vessel had grounded at high water and was hard and fast, the tugs could not move her. Life Savers landed the Captain, his wife and four children and the crew of 19. The seas continued to be too rough for salvage and much of the cargo was lost. A company of wreckers succeeded in floating the ship on the 15th and towed her to Portland for repairs. *Photo courtesy of the Kennebunkport Historical Society.*

The legend of the wreck of the Annie C. McGuire (sic) is painted on a rock opposite the Portland Head Lighthouse. *Photo by William P. Quinn.*

A strange and mysterious legend in Maine is about the Dead Ship of Harpswell. The story has passed down from generation to generation and tells of a full rigged ship with all sails set coming into the bay just after sunset. There are different versions of the tale where the ship is a derelict or a ghost vessel sailing out of the fog with a dead crew. Many believe the ship exists and appears now and then along the coast trying to return to Harpswell. John Greenleaf Whittier, the noted poet, wrote an eerie verse on the subject:

THE DEAD SHIP OF HARPSWELL
By John Greenleaf Whittier

What flecks the outer gray beyond
  The sundown's golden trail?
The white flash of a sea-bird's wing,
  Or gleam of slanting sail?
Let young eyes watch from Neck and Point,
  And sea-worn elders pray,—
The ghost of what was once a ship
  Is sailing up the bay!

From gray sea-fog, from icy drift,
  From peril and from pain,
The home-bound fisher greets thy lights,
  O hundred-harbored Maine!
But many a keel shall seaward turn,
  And many a sail outstand,
When, tall and white, the Dead Ship looms
  Against the dusk of land.

She rounds the headland's bristling pines;
  She threads the isle-set bay;
No spur of breeze can speed her on,
  Nor ebb of tide delay.
Old men still walk the Isle of Orr
  Who tell her date and name,
Old shipwrights sit in Freeport yards
  Who hewed her oaken frame.

What weary doom of baffled quest,
  Thou sad sea-ghost, is thine?
What makes thee in the haunts of home
  A winder and a sign?
No foot is on thy silent deck,
  Upon thy helm no hand;
No ripple hath the soundless wind
  That smites thee from the land!

For never comes the ship to port,
  Howe'er the breeze may be;
Just when she nears the waiting shore
  She drifts again to sea.
No tack of sail, nor turn of helm,
  Nor sheer of veering side;
Stern-fore she drives to sea and night,
  Against the wind and tide.

In vain o'er Harpswell Neck the star
  Of evening guides her in;
In vain for her the lamps are lit
  Within thy tower, Seguin!
In vain the harbor-boat shall hail,
  In vain the pilot call;
No hand shall reef her spectral sail,
  Or let her anchor fall.

Shake, brown old wives, with dreary joy,
  Your gray-head hints of ill;
And, over sick-beds whispering low,
  Your prophecies fulfil.
Some home amid yon birchen trees
  Shall drape its door with woe;
And slowly where the Dead Ship sails,
  The burial boat shall row!

From Wolf Neck and from Flying Point,
  From island and from main,
From sheltered cove and tided creek,
  Shall glide the funeral train.
The dead-boat with the bearers four,
  The mourners at her stern,—
And one shall go the silent way
  Who shall no more return!

And men shall sigh, and women weep,
  Whose dear ones pale and pine,
And sadly over sunset seas
  Await the ghostly sign.
They know not that its sails are filled
  By pity's tender breath,
Nor see the Angel at the helm
  Who steers the Ship of Death!

The Life Saving Service was called on for various types of rescues from the many different wrecks along the Maine Coast. On January 9, 1880, the schooner *Mateira* capsized off Green Point, a mile west of Quoddy Light. The Life Savers of the West Quoddy Head station launched their surfboat and rowed to the vessel and found her on her beam ends and the crew of five clinging to the side of the schooner with heavy seas threatening to sweep them off. They were rescued by the Lifesavers and taken to the station and treated for exposure and exhaustion and provided with dry clothes. Later the schooner drifted ashore but all that could be saved was her sails and part of the rigging. Some of the personal effects of the crew were also saved.

During a fierce easterly gale and snowstorm the British bark *Scotia,* 921 tons, from Bahia, Brazil to St. John, N.B., lost spars and canvas and was wrecked one mile southeast of the West Quoddy Head station early in the morning of December 15, 1882. Life Savers went immediately to the scene and the first shot from the wreck gun carried the line directly over the vessel. Captain Andrew M. Foster of the *Scotia* quickly had the hawser fast and by 7 a.m., the Life Savers had sent the breeches-buoy off to the vessel. The crewmen came ashore two at a time in the buoy and after all had landed, Captain Foster was reluctant to leave his vessel. Keeper Myers went offshore in the buoy and advised the Captain to leave and save his life. After the storm abated, they could save the ship and her property if conditions permitted. Captain Foster took the good advice of the Keeper and came ashore. The bark became a total loss although later in the day with a shift of wind, the sea subsided sufficiently to permit the surfmen to go off in their boat and save some of the crew's clothing and the Captain's charts and instruments.

The brig *Dart* of Halifax, Nova Scotia on a passage from Lisbon, Portugal to Calais in ballast ran on a ledge of rocks a quarter mile southwest of the Crumple Island Life Saving Station in dense fog. The accident occurred on September 6, 1886. The surfmen launched their boat and quickly removed the passengers. The vessel swerved around on the rocks and stove in her hull planks and quickly filled with water. After landing the passengers the Life Savers returned and took off the crew. They saved the personal property of the passengers and crew but the hull was a total loss.

When the sun and the moon are in conjunction or in opposition, their combined action creates an extra high tide along the coast usually called a spring tide. During a spring tide on June 26, 1889, the three master schooner *William C. French* went up on Glovers Rock, six miles southwest of the Hunniwells Beach Life Saving Station. This was the inactive season and the Keeper had to summon part of the crew from their homes. Together with volunteers, they launched the surfboat and rowed to the scene of the wreck. After they have rowed a while, a tug came along and gave them a tow to the disabled craft. The ship was bound from Boston, Massachusetts to Boothbay and had stranded at midnight in dense fog. Repeated attempts to pull the schooner off the rock failed and the vessel was abandoned and subsequently sold at public auction. The Sewall Company of Bath bought her "as is". They jacked her up and built a new ways under her and launched her as they would a new ship. Her new name was *Dicky Bird* because she had perched on land.

The life of a surfman in the Life Saving Service was periods of long dull duty with watch standing and tedious patrols up and down the coast. But every vestige of monotony was erased when the crew was called out to a wreck. On the night of October 27, 1889, the schooner *Frank Maria,* of Ellsworth lost her way in a storm and drove on to Odiorne's Point near Portsmouth, New Hampshire. With the vessel in among the rocks and the waves breaking over her, the crew climbed into the rigging to keep from being swept away. There was no way to signal for help from shore so the men began to shout as loud as they could in hopes that someone would hear them. The yells were heard by persons on shore and the Life Savers from the Jerrys Point station were summoned.

The Life Savers launched their boat and rowed to the scene but due to the darkness it was difficult to know how to approach the rocky area around the wreck. In a hazardous move, the Keeper ran his boat in alongside the wreck and somehow managed to take three men out of the rigging and into his boat. Heavy swells pushed the boat away from the wreck and the last man leaped into the water and was quickly picked up by the Life Savers. A light from shore was shown to guide the surfmen back to safety. They brought the four survivors to the station for dry clothes and warm food and drink. The schooner was a total loss.

CHAPTER THREE

At the end of the 19th century, Maine was one of the busiest maritime commerce areas on the east coast of the United States. The history of Maine's economic development is directly related to the development of the shipbuilding industry. After Maine became a state in 1820, there was an extraordinary growth in the economy. Shipbuilding and lumbering prospered early, followed by the lime trade, ice harvesting and granite quarrying. In the second half of the century, manufacturing of textiles, paper and leather products grew to be important cogs in the economic gears in addition to the fishing and farming that was carried on state wide. An unwelcome aspect of this was the numerous wrecks that followed the business boom.

The lumbering industry began early, about the middle of the 17th century when the English started cutting tall timber for ships' masts. The great rivers of Maine that emptied into the Atlantic were the scene of the lumber bonanza in later years. Millions of board feet of lumber, lath and shingles supplied cargoes for the sailing vessels. Another profitable but dangerous cargo was lime. The chief port for lime was Rockland. The primary vessel used was the two masted schooner. The main hazzard was fire. Usually, old worn out schooners were used as limers, and they leaked. When water came in contact with the lime casks, the resulting fire most always consumed the vessel.

During the cold winter months, the Kennebec River freezes. The ice is between one and two feet thick. In the late 19th century, the banks of the Kennebec were lined with ice houses. The ice was harvested and stored during the cold months. In May, the first schooners began to come up river to load ice for the southern ports. Overseas, ice was more profitable than lumber. In 1920, artificial ice making and the refrigerator cooled the Maine ice industry. The rivers still freeze in winter but today, the ice houses are gone and the ice just melts in the spring. The granite industry followed along the same pattern as ice. The first quarrying began early in the 1800's and later the business boomed. But right after 1900, it died out with the development of concrete. As in the lime trades, old worn out vessels were used to carry the extremely heavy cargo and wrecks were frequent. Many famous buildings all over the United States are made from granite quarried from the islands in Maine's Penobscot Bay.

In 1790, Alexander Hamilton asked Congress for ten boats to launch the U.S. Revenue Marine to enforce the country's law on the high seas. Winter cruises began in 1831 giving aid to persons in distress at sea, preserving property and saving cargoes of wrecked vessels. In the long history of the service, Revenue cutters have a proud record of rescues and devotion to duty and have fought alongside the U.S. Naval vessels in time of war.

On January 12, 1891, the U.S. Revenue Cutter *Woodbury* was waiting out a storm in Rockland Harbor. The vessel got underway following the gale and steamed through fog to search for vessels in distress. Out in Casco Bay shortly after noon a signal was discovered from the Junk of Pork Rock near Outer Green Island. Upon inspection of the area, the remains of a wrecked vessel were discovered in the breakers and clinging to the rock, just out of reach of the towering waves were six shipwrecked men.

A heavy southeast sea was running and the area was surrounded by jagged boulders and spurs. Breakers about 30 feet high were smashing against the rock the men were hanging on, making a boat landing all but impossible. The cutter *Woodbury* remained steaming around the rock all day to encourage the imperiled crew, hoping that the sea would abate enough to enable the cutter to drift a line to the rock and pull the men off through the breakers. Darkness fell and the cutter departed the scene and proceeded to Portland in order to obtain two dories from a fishing vessel and inform the Cape Elizabeth Life Saving station of the wreck.

The cutter departed Portland early the next morning and was on scene at first light. Overnight the wind had backed around to the west and the seas were reduced considerably. The two dories and a boat were launched from the *Woodbury* and rowed to the rock to effect a rescue. At this time, the boat from the Life Saving Station arrived to assist in the rescue. With excellent boat handling, all six men were rescued from the rock and taken aboard the Revenue cutter and cared for, fed and given dry clothes. The cutter then proceeded to Portland with the rescued men.

Above: The schooner *Empress* from New York to Kennebunkport with a cargo of coal went ashore on Fox Point at the mouth of the Kennebunk River on October 28, 1891. The hull heeled over at low tide and became a total loss on the rocks. **Below:** The hull of the *Empress* lay on the rocks for a few days and on November 6th she broke in half and drifted nearer shore. The hull was sold to a wrecking company. *Photos courtesy of the Kennebunkport Historical Society.*

Above: The Kennebunkport Historical Society has preserved part of the *Empress*. Russell Bryant holds the battered quarterboard of the wrecked ship. *Photo by William P. Quinn.* **Below:** The American schooner *Erie* stranded off Jonesport on December 28, 1894. The Life Savers boarded the beached vessel and helped man her pumps. The schooner was pulled off the rocks but was badly damaged. *Photo courtesy of Capt. W.J.L. Parker, U.S.C.G. (Ret.).*

The four masted schooner *Katie J. Barrett,* with a cargo of Kennebec River ice went aground on Cape Cod during a storm on February 16, 1890. Cape Cod Life Savers launched a surfboat and rowed through heavy surf and high winds to rescue the crew. The vessel lay on Nauset Bar in Orleans, Mass., for seven months before the hull was refloated. *Photo by Henry K. Cummings, Orleans, Mass.*

Above: The U.S. Lighthouse supply steamer *Armeria* cruising in fog in East Penobscot Bay on August 15, 1897 ran up on a large ledge of rocks north of Bradbury Island. The tide was high at the time and there were rocks amidship. At low tide her stern was out of water. **Below:** Wreckers had to use pontoons to float her on the 23rd. The U.S. Steamers *Lilac* and *Myrtle* and tugs *Ralph Ross, Kate Jones* and *William Sprague,* pulled the *Armeria* off the rocks and towed her into Northwest Harbor. *Photos from the marine collection of Frank E. Claes, Orland, Maine.*

Above: In October of 1899 the coastal steamer *Cimbria* of the Bangor and Bar Harbor Steamboat Company ran up on the rocks in the fog at Bass Harbor on the southeast point of Mount Desert Island. *Photo courtesy of W.H. Ballard.* **Below:** The vessel lay on the rocks at low tide and was pulled off badly damaged. She had to be rebuilt and in the spring of 1900 was re-launched with a new superstructure but minus her two masts. *Photo from the collection of Frank E. Claes, Orland, Maine.*

Above: The battleship *Maine,* built in 1888 of 6,682 tons with four 10″ and six 6″ guns. She was listed as one of the first class vessels in the United States Navy. The ship was in Havana Harbor to protect American interests in Cuba. On February 15, 1898, a mysterious explosion sunk the ship and killed 266 men. There were many questions as to the cause. The Americans blamed the Spanish and the Spanish claimed that the Americans deliberately scuttled the ship to provoke a war. In April, the United States declared war on Spain. The U.S. won the war which lasted until August and finally ended with the treaty of Paris. The *Maine,* however, was not remembered until long after the war. **Below:** Increased traffic in Havana Harbor produced demands to remove the wreck which was a menace to navigation. After she was raised in 1911, it was discovered that the explosion that sank her was from an external source, indicating that a mine and not internal sabotage, sank the *Maine.* The hull was towed out and sunk in the Gulf of Mexico in 600 fathoms of water. *Photos from the collection of Paul C. Morris, Nantucket, Mass.*

THE PORTLAND GALE

One of the most dangerous storms ever recorded occurred on November 26 and 27, in 1898. The two day hurricane is commonly referred to as the Portland Gale after the famous steamer that was lost with all hands. The blizzard raged for over thirty-six hours and wrecked ships all along the New England coast from Eastport to Block Island. Seventy mile-an-hour winds and mountainous seas tossed ships up on the shore like driftwood. The U.S. Life Saving Service annual report lists fifty vessels in distress along the shorelines. Twice that number were wrecked or damaged where the Life Savers could not reach them. The storm wrecked more ships than any other in our history. The aftermath was appalling. Several ships did not report at all, indicating a loss at sea. The shoreline geography was altered by the force of the hurricane. Communications were cut off from outlying areas such as Cape Cod where news of the Portland wreckage was flashed over transatlantic wires to France and then back over another wire to New York and thence to Boston.

The steamer *Portland* was bound from Boston, Massachusetts to her home port in Portland, Maine. She was lost somewhere off Cape Cod with all her crew and passengers (estimated at close to 200 persons, most of whom were from Maine). The exact number was not known, as the Purser failed to turn in the passenger count to boatline officials prior to sailing. The ship left the dock at 7 p.m. with a full load of Thanksgiving Holiday passengers on their way back to Portland. There has been much controversy as to why Captain Horace H. Blanchard took his ship out that evening. Arguments pro and con have been debated for years. What is known for sure is that her wreckage and many bodies washed up on shore between Peaked Hill Bars and Highland Light on Cape Cod. This factor would place the shipwreck northeast of Cape Cod when she went down.

The great gale of November 1898 sank the steamer *Portland* and all her crew and passengers, nearly 200 persons. The ship went down off Cape Cod. *Photo courtesy of the Peabody Museum of Salem.*

This artist's conception of the loss of the Portland tries to depict the violence of the storm. While it is doubtful a lifeboat could be launched in this sea, artist's license lays the ship in the trough of the sea which would surely capsize her. There were no survivors to tell the true story of what happened. *Photo courtesy of the Allie Ryan Collection at the Maine Maritime Academy in Castine.*

In 1945, the late Edward Rowe Snow, noted historian, announced that the wreckage of the *Portland* had been discovered nine miles northeast of Cape Cod in 22 fathoms of water. It was located by Captain Charles B. Carver of Rockland, Maine, whose scallop dragger picked up a bell that was later identified as coming from the ill fated ship. Dives were made to the wreckage in that area but nothing definite was established. After a few years on the bottom, most of the wooden hull would be pretty well rotted. The metal machinery, while still intact, would deteriorate. Modern electronics such as side scan sonar could establish the exact location of the *Portland* if and when it is found.

The tragic result of the loss of the *Portland* was evident in the headlines. An example was the Portland Evening Express of November 29, 1898:

THE LAST HOPE IS NOW GONE

THE STEAMER PORTLAND IS SURELY LOST

GLOOM CAST OVER PORTLAND

The story gives the details of the bodies and wreckage cast upon the shores of Cape Cod. The suspense and anxiety of loved ones waiting for those who would never return and conjecture on the Captain's decision to sail that night, followed by the list of persons believed to be on board the steamship. Most of the names were taken from a list of those relatives who called the ship's office to inquire as to the fate of the vessel.

Above: The wreckage from the steamer *Portland* washed ashore on the backside of Cape Cod between Peaked Hill Bars and Highland Light. Stair railings, cabin doors, life jackets, life boat oars, deck chairs and a quarterboard were set up and photographed for the record. *Photo courtesy of Cape Cod Photos, Orleans, Mass.* **Below Right:** The Portland Plaque, attached to the side of the Highland Lighthouse in Truro. **Below Left:** This is a reproduction of the ship-card of the steamer *Portland* and her sister ship the *Bay State*. *Photo courtesy of Gordon Caldwell, Hyannis, Mass.*

28

On October 13, 1898, the lime schooner *Cyrus Chamberlain* anchored off Clark's Island in Portsmouth, N.H., harbor. Her cargo had caught fire and the crew was attempting to seal the hold and smother the fire. The Keeper and crew of the Jerrys Point Life Saving Station pulled out to the schooner but the Captain declined assistance and said that the fire was under control. The next day, the Keeper was notified that help was needed. The surfmen again pulled to the vessel and found that the fire was out of control and it was impossible to save the schooner. The Life Savers assisted the crew, hove up the anchor and grounded the burning vessel on the flats. They helped strip her of all salvagable gear. The schooner was a total loss.

The schooner *Eva May* ashore at Old Orchard Beach around the turn of the century. *Photo from the collection of Roger Peterson, Cape Elizabeth, Maine.*

Above: The *Fannie and Edith* wrecked on Prout's Neck in Scarborough on December 4, 1900. *Photo from the collection of Roger Peterson, Cape Elizabeth, Maine.* **Below:** Photographic reproduction of the watercolor "The Wrecked Schooner" by Winslow Homer, noted Maine artist. The wreck depicted was that of the *Fanny and Edith*. *Photo courtesy The St. Louis Art Museum.*

CHAPTER FOUR

The turn of the century ushered in a new era with new ideas. Automobiles were becoming popular and would ultimately become the most important factor in the U.S. economy. They were not built in Maine however; Detroit was the natural location for manufacture. It was near the iron ore and steel needed to build engines. Henry Ford and Ransom Olds opened up production lines and the automobile was on the road. There was no immediate effect, but the cars and then the paved roads would later cause the demise of the Maine coastal steamers. Other transportation pioneers were the Wright Brothers who made the first powered flight at Kill Devil Hills, at Cape Hatteras in North Carolina in December, 1903. An interesting sidelight in this initial effort into aviation was the assistance of the surfmen of the Kill Devil Hills Life Boat Station. They served as the amateur ground crew for the Wright Brothers when they made their famous flight.

Another invention with a decided effect on shipping was the development of the radio. Inventor Guglielmo Marconi had improved the equipment so that he could send messages across the Atlantic Ocean in 1903. The first rescue made as a result of the wireless was on January 23, 1909, twenty-six miles south of Nantucket Island when the Italian liner *Florida* rammed into the side of the British steamer *Republic*. SOS messages brought aid to both vessels. The steamer *Baltic* rescued 1,650 passengers from the two ships. The *Florida* limped into port but the *Republic* sank in 50 fathoms of water. Without the radio, the death toll would have been appalling.

During a strong gale with heavy rain, the steamer *Californian* stranded on Ram Island Ledge just outside Portland harbor. The steamer had just cleared Portland harbor on her way to Halifax. The grounding occurred at 2:30 a.m. on February 25, 1900. Surfmen from the Cape Elizabeth Life Saving Station spotted her just after daylight. They launched the surfboat and after a difficult pull, they reached the side of the steamer. The sight of the surfmen being tossed about in the rough seas was enough to convince the passengers and crewmen of the steamer to remain on board. The Life Savers returned to their station. The surfmen rowed to the wreck again the next day and assisted in the transfer of passengers and baggage to a small steamer alongside the grounded liner. The *Californian* was later turned over to the wreckers. Two attempts were made to pull her off the ledge but she would not budge. After the $300,000 cargo was removed, the vessel was pulled off on April 1st and beached on the flats. She was patched up and then taken to Boston for an overhaul.

On August 11, 1901, the Cape Elizabeth Life Savers assisted in saving the American Barkentine *Jessie MacGregor* when she was carried onto Aldens Rock while sailing into Portland harbor. The breeze was light and the vessel would not answer her helm. The surfmen rowed out to her and found a tugboat alongside. They went aboard and assisted the crew on the pumps. The vessel was towed into the harbor and safely berthed at the dock. The barkentine was of 608 tons, from Philadelphia to Portland with a crew of eight and a cargo of coal.

In early December 1900, gale winds lashed the coast and the two masted schooner *Fanny and Edith* ran in behind Richmond Island to escape the brunt of the storm. Later that evening the winds increased and the little schooner parted her cables and went adrift. She was blown across the bay and was cast ashore on the east side of Prouts Neck. The crew managed to make it ashore safely but the vessel was in a bad place. There were photographs made of the schooner before she broke up. One of these was used by Winslow Homer to create the water color "The Wrecked Schooner." Winslow Homer, 1836-1910 spent his summers at Prouts Neck. In his later life, he painted some striking seascapes of the Maine Coast. The water color of the *Fanny and Edith* is an excellent representation of the trauma and adversity of a shipwreck.

Five months after the *Fanny and Edith* was wrecked, a more serious wreck occurred at Broad Cove on Cape Elizabeth, where three men drowned. The 99 ton Canadian schooner *Wendell Burpee* was from New York City to St. John, N.B., with a cargo of 153 tons of coal. On April 7, 1901, the schooner was running with only the standing jib before the storm. Captain Lewis Meresburg sighted two lights which he thought marked Matinicus Rock. He soon discovered his error and with the weather raining and misty with a heavy sea running, he decided to make an effort to run into Portland Harbor. The Life Savers at Cape Elizabeth had the schooner under surveillance, and, when the crew could not control the vessel, they began a rescue effort.

The vessel anchored in Broad Cove and the Keeper ordered the beach cart manned. Soon after, the anchor chain parted and the schooner was drifting helplessly, stern first, onto the beach. When the Life Savers arrived at the scene, they found that they were too late. The crew of the schooner had left their vessel in the yawl boat which had capsized. Only one man was able to swim ashore, the mate John Swenson. As fate would have it, the Life Safers could have saved all on board had they stayed with their vessel. Subsequently, one body was found. The other two were never recovered.

At the entrance to the Kennebec River on the east side lies Whale Back Rock. Eight feet high and bare, the rock is situated about a half mile east of Pond Island. A shoal extends 100 yards southward from it and is dangerous for sailing vessels. On May 2, 1890, the brig *Charles Dennis* of Bath was entering the Kennebec River when the wind died. The current carried the brig onto Whale Back Rock where she was wrecked. The brig's crew of eight men took to their boat while the Keeper and surfmen of the Hunniwell's Beach Life Saving Station launched their surfboat and went out to assist the shipwrecked crew. The heavy seas began to break up the vessel and the Life Savers picked up small articles in the water. They escorted the crew to the station where they were made comfortable. The brig was a total loss.

About ten years later, another vessel was wrecked on Whale Back Rock. The schooner *Joseph Luther* with a crew of seven, bound from Bath to Clarks Cove, Maine under her master John Francis. On January 21, 1901, the schooner was being towed out of the Kennebec and she was just to the windward of Whale Back Rock when the hawser parted and she drifted onto the rocks. Surfmen from the Hunniwell's Beach Life Saving Station pulled out at once but were unable to go alongside because of the heavy swells breaking near the rock. The Keeper pulled to the leeward of the rocks and managed to land a surfman, who threw a line to the wreck and made the end fast to a rock. The men from the wreck came down the line and with much difficulty were taken aboard the lifeboat. After the shipwrecked men were rescued, they were taken to the station and provided with dry clothing and warm food. The schooner was a total loss.

The Hunniwells Beach surfmen in a lifeboat drill in the Kennebec River with Keeper Harvey Berry at the steering oar. *Photo, circa 1903-04, by Capt. Jim Perkins, courtesy of Jane Stevens, Bath, Maine.*

Above: On the afternoon of January 21, 1901, the 422 ton schooner *Joseph Luther* went up on Whale Back Rock at the entrance to the Kennebec River. Life Savers from the Hunniwell's Beach Life Saving Station saved the seven man crew but the schooner was a total loss. **Below:** After a couple of storms the hull of the *Joseph Luther* split in half. Wreckers stripped her of all salvageable gear and the ocean claimed the rest. *Photos by Capt. James Perkins, courtesy of Jane W. Stevens, Bath, Maine.*

A new boat on the line was always a thing of beauty and wonder. On June 10, 1894, the *City of Bangor* made her first run to Maine. She was a good sea boat, dependable, with speed and luxury. She was able to make three trips a week between Boston and Bangor. Her popularity gained her the nickname "The Floating Goldmine." The steamer suffered a few accidents in her 30 year career in Maine waters. In 1902, she struck Monhegan Island in dense fog and had to be beached at Sprucehead Island. In 1906, she was in collision with the steamer *City of Rockland*. In 1913, her worst experience was a fire at the dock in Boston which almost finished her and took the life of one crewman. Her last trip to Maine was in 1924. In 1927, she was retired and laid alongside the old four master schooner *Snetind* at Federal Wharf in East Boston. On December 27, 1933, she developed a list under tons of snow. Water poured into her hull and she sank. The years passed and she went down into the mud out of sight. The *City of Bangor* lies in a shallow grave in East Boston, Massachusetts.

In June 1906 the *City of Bangor* was in collision with her sister ship the *City of Rockland* off Portland and suffered the loss of part of her bow.
Photo from the marine collection of Frank E. Claes, Orland, Maine.

Above: On September 28, 1902 the *City of Bangor* struck on Monhegan Island in thick fog and was later beached at Lobster Cove on Spruce Head Island to prevent her from sinking. Temporary repairs were made and she steamed to Boston under her own power for overhaul. *Photo from the Ballard Collection at the Bath Marine Museum.* **Below:** The *City of Bangor* finished her days at Federal Wharf in East Boston when she sank on December 27, 1933, beside the four masted schooner *Snetind*. She went out of documentation in 1935 and was abandoned where she lay. *Photo by R. Loren Graham courtesy of S.H.S. of America.*

Above: A multitude of natural hazards caused the steamer *Penobscot* to go aground on February 28, 1903. The vessel was feeling her way up river in a dense fog, against the tide and stiff winds causing a heavy swell. She veered from her course and struck on Odom's Ledge, five miles below Bucksport on the Penobscot River. The steamer was pulled off the next day with minor damage. *Photo courtesy of Allie Ryan, Brooksville, Maine.*
Below: On December 5, 1901 the Gloucester fishing vessel *Mary A. Brown* stranded at Great Boars Head at Hampton Beach, New Hampshire. The schooner was of 15 tons with a crew of 5, all of which were lost. Her wreckage lay on the beach and a sign was posted on the mast. The photograph is a reproduction of a tinted post card on which the date is wrong.

Hampton Beach, N.H., Wreck of Schooner Mary A Brown.

Wreck of Sadie and Lillie, September 17, 1903, at Pemaquid Point, Me.

Above: A September storm of unprecedented violence smashed the Maine coast in 1903 leaving death and destruction in its wake. Dozens of vessels were seriously damaged and two were totally wrecked with tragic results. The schooners *George L. Emunds* of Gloucester with a crew of 16 and the *Sadie and Lillie* of Machias with a crew of 3 were both wrecked on the treacherous bar at the end of Pemaquid Point with an appalling loss of life. Fifteen men were lost that night, 14 from the *George L. Emunds* and 1 from the *Sadie and Lillie*. The *Emunds* went on the rocks and broke up. The crew, mostly from Gloucester, launched their dories but they were smashed to pieces on the rocks as soon as they were in the water. The crew succeeded in launching one boat and five men started the hazardous journey toward shore. They were half way in when a huge wave capsized the small craft. The five men began the long swim towards shore but only two of them reached their goal and they were more dead than alive when pulled out of the water. They were the only two survivors from the *George L. Emunds*. One Maine man was lost in the rescue of the crew of the *Sadie and Lillie* when she piled up on the rocks. The photograph is a reproduction of a post card depicting the wreck of the *Sadie and Lillie*. **Below:** The death of a beautiful sailing ship is a tragic loss to her owners. The largest ship ever built in Maine was the *Henry B. Hyde*. Built in Bath in 1884, of 2,583 tons and launched November 5th; the ship had many mishaps during her career. Fires, collisions etc. but the end came on February 11, 1904 while under tow from New York to Baltimore she broke loose from the tug in a gale and went ashore. She was later floated but again stranded on Virginia Beach and broke in two in another storm on October 4th. *Photo courtesy of the Mariners Museum, Newport News, Virginia.*

The five master schooner *Washington B. Thomas* was launched in April, 1903 at Thomaston and had the shortest sailing career of any of the big schooners. She only lasted two months. Bound for Portland with 4,226 tons of coal, the vessel anchored off shore in calm but foggy weather on June 11, 1903. The next day, a southeast wind freshened and the seas picked up and the vessel was discovered to have dragged anchor. The storm later intensified to gale force and Captain William J. Lermond decided to make sail and beat out to sea to ride out the storm.

There was difficulty in raising a second anchor and big seas were breaking over the schooner. At this time she was carried on to the reefs off Stratton's Island. The huge vessel started to break up and the Captain went aft to get his wife from the cabin which was flooded. He was unsuccessful and the woman died when she was struck on the head by a falling beam. The crew at this time had all climbed into the rigging to await rescue. They assisted Captain Lermond onto the spanker boom as the stern part of the ship washed away with Mrs. Lermond's body and at the same time spilling her cargo of coal into the sea. Because of the thick fog and heavy rain and stormy conditions prevailing at the time, the men were not seen until the next day. News of the wreck reached the Life Saving Station at Cape Elizabeth but as this was the inactive season, Keeper Dyer had to secure volunteers to supplement his limited crew. The substitute crew rowed out to the wreck in mountainous seas and rescued nine of the fourteen men in the rigging. The boat at that time was overloaded and the surfmen return to shore. The sea conditions at the time made it dangerous for them to return and they decided to wait until the next day to effect the rescue of the remainder of the crew. The remaining five men spent another stormy night holding on for their lives in the rigging. The surfmen returned early the next morning and found the seas had calmed enough to take the last of the shipwrecked men off the ship. Many of the crew had been badly injured and required medical attention when they reached shore. The body of Mrs. Lermond washed ashore a few days later on Cape Elizabeth. The wrecked schooner broke up and was a total loss.

The five masted schooner *Washington B. Thomas* on her launch day in April, 1903 at Thomaston, with flags flying and a large party aboard. The vessel had a short career in the coal trades. *Photo from the collection of Paul C. Morris, Nantucket, Mass.*

A drawing of the wreck of the *Washington B. Thomas* on the ledges off Strattons Island on June 12, 1903. The life savers in the surfboat are fighting mountainous seas to effect the rescue of the crew of the ill-fated schooner. *Drawing by Paul C. Morris, Nantucket, Mass.*

The two masted schooner *Lizzie Carr* was wrecked on Foss Ledge off Rye, New Hampshire on January 7, 1905, with the loss of one life. The schooner was of 286 tons from Calais to New York City with a cargo of lumber. She was anchored off shore when a southeast gale and heavy seas dragged her anchors and she parted her chains. Plunging stern first, she struck on the rocky ledge about 250 yards off shore. Her masts fell when she struck, carrying down crewmen who had been driven aloft by the heavy seas sweeping her decks. Her cargo of lumber washed out and drifted in piles in the surf and was scattered about making rescue of the crewmen difficult if not almost impossible. The Life Savers from the Wallis Sands Station were on the scene with the beach cart and a shot line was fired out over the wreck. The line became fouled in the mass of wreckstuff between the schooner and the shore.

At this point, the men tried to launch their surfboat but the seas cast them back ashore. The sea was so full of wreckage it seemed that any rescue effort would be in vain but surfmen from the Rye and Jerrys Point stations arrived at the wreck site to assist. A picked crew of three keepers and four expert surfmen manned the boat. They managed to get the boat off the beach and through the surf. There were many obstacles going off shore to reach the stranded crewmen. After a long and hazardous pull, the Life Savers reached the wreck and picked off six men clinging to the top of the deck house, one by one, in high seas. Some of the crew had been badly injured in their fall. One had a broken leg and the others were badly bruised by their ordeal. The Life Savers brought the boat through the wreckage to shore where the other surfmen aided in bringing the boat to land. The Life Savers had carried out a miraculous rescue and when they arrived on shore they learned that the Mate of the ill-fated schooner had attempted to reach shore on some floating timber shortly after the vessel struck but the sea washed him away and he disappeared. His body was never found.

The U.S. Life Saving Service crew and lifeboat effecting a rescue of the crew of the schooner *Lizzie Carr* during a storm on January 7, 1905, off Rye, New Hampshire. *Photo from the collection of William Varrell, courtesy of the Mariners Museum, Newport News, Virginia.*

Above: The power of the ocean is vividly displayed in this photograph of the remains of the lumber schooner *Lizzie Carr* after her wreck off Rye, New Hampshire. *Photo from the collection of William Varrell, courtesy of the Mariners Museum, Newport News, Va.* **Below:** At Fiddlers Reach on the Kennebec River, just south of Bath, the *Ransom B. Fuller* went aground early in the morning of August 19, 1905 in thick fog. The steamer was stuck until high tide, later in the day, when she floated off. *Photo by James Perkins, courtesy of Jane Stevens, Bath, Maine.*

Above: The elegant steamer *City of Rockland* had an unfortunate accident early in her career. On the morning of July 26, 1904 she was steaming through dense fog when she struck Upper Gangway Ledge in the Muscle Ridge Channel. The impact broke her main steam pipe and she remained without power for a short while. The vessel floated off with the rising tide and drifted about two miles and fetched up atop another wreck on Grindstone Ledge. **Below:** Her 400 passengers were taken off by other Penobscot Bay steamers while the surfmen from the White Head Life Saving Station assisted the crew and transferred the baggage and cargo. Later, salvage vessels pumped her out and brought her to Rockland for temporary repairs. She was then towed to Boston for extensive rebuilding. *Photos courtesy of Steven Lang, Owls Head, Maine.*

Above: On September 1, 1906 the schooner *Annie L. Henderson* was at the dock at Bangor, Maine. It was mid-morning and workmen were unloading her cargo of coal when a fire broke out in a shed on the pier. The flames spread to the schooner before she could cast off. Stiff winds fanned the fire and soon the vessel was ablaze from stem to stern. The Bangor Fire Department was summoned and they managed to confine the fire on the dock but could not reach the schooner which had been blown across the river toward Brewer. Later the vessel was towed to mid-stream and she burned to the water line and was a total loss. *Photo from the marine collection of Frank E. Claes, Orland, Maine.* **Below:** The Canadian schooner *Bessie Parker* was wrecked on the beach 1½ miles southwest of the West Quoddy Life Saving Station on October 7, 1906. During a heavy wind and high seas the vessel drifted onto the beach. Surfmen manned their surfboat and went alongside to render assistance. The crew of six was removed and the Life Savers saved personal effects and aided the crew in stripping the schooner. The vessel was of 240 tons out of St. John, N.B. for New York with a cargo of lath. The schooner was a total loss. *Photo courtesy of the Mariners Museum, Newport News, Virginia.*

Above: A heavy northwest gale grounded the four master schooner *Helen B. Crosby* on Drunkard Ledge off North Haven Island on October 11, 1906. The vessel with a cargo of coal was damaged beyond repair and she broke up early in November. *Photo courtesy of Capt. W.J.L. Parker, U.S.C.G (Ret.).* **Below:** The three masted schooner *Ellen M. Mitchell* stranded on the rocks at Jonesport at 3:45 a.m. on May 16, 1907. When the surfmen from the Great Wass Island station boarded her she was full of water and fast on the rocks. The Life Savers rescued the crew and landed their gear. The *Ellen M. Mitchell* was of 379 tons from St. John, N.B. to New York City with a cargo of lumber. She was a total loss. *Photo from the collection of Frank Claes, Orland, Maine.*

Above: The freight steamer *Massasoit* of the Maine Coast Transportation Co., was battling gale winds while on her way from Lubec to Boston on January 8, 1908 when she was blown ashore at Cutler. The vessel was carried high on the beach and the salvage effort had to wait for two weeks for another run of high tides. There were no injuries except to the hull of the steamer. A portion of the keel was damaged when she grounded on the rocky coast. Repairs were made and the freight removed. The steamer was pulled off the beach on February 3rd by the cutter *Woodbury* and towed to Portland. *Photo from the marine collection of Frank Claes, Orland, Maine.* **Below:** On June 1, 1908, the steamer *Boothbay* caught her port guard on the wharf during a night tide, listed to starboard and had water flow into her ports. A salvage lighter is alongside and a diver is down sealing the hull prior to pumping. It took three weeks to raise her and then she had to be rebuilt. The steamer *Camden* is in the background. *Photo courtesy of the Bath Marine Museum, Bath, Maine.*

Above: On July 1, 1909 the four masted schooner *Alice E. Clark* was sailing up in Penobscot Bay on a fine afternoon bound for Bangor with 2,700 tons of coal. Her Captain apparently misjudged her location and the vessel ran up on Coomb's Ledge off the east shore of Islesboro. The sharp ledge pierced the schooner's hull and she sank by the stern. **Below:** Extensive salvage efforts failed and the hull broke up in a storm in December. *Photos from the collection of Paul C. Morris, Nantucket, Massachusetts.*

46

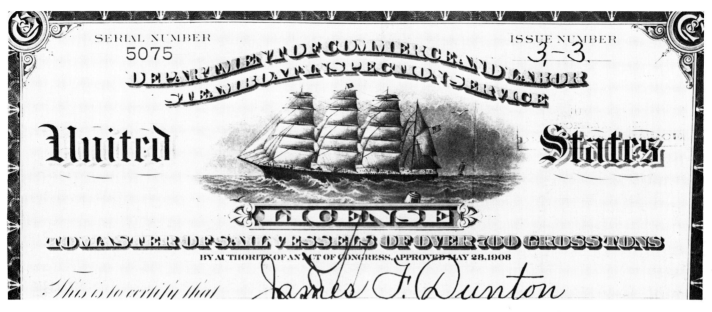

SERIAL NUMBER
5075

ISSUE NUMBER
3–3.

DEPARTMENT OF COMMERCE AND LABOR
STEAMBOAT INSPECTION SERVICE

United States

LICENSE

TO MASTER OF SAIL VESSELS OF OVER 700 GROSS TONS

BY AUTHORITY OF AN ACT OF CONGRESS, APPROVED MAY 28, 1908

This is to certify that James F. Dunton

The Captain's license for a master of sailing vessels of over 700 gross tons proudly displayed the illustration of the Bath built *Shenendoah*. A close look will reveal the Sewall house flag with the "S" plainly visible atop the main mast. *Courtesy of the Maine Maritime Museum at Bath.*

CHAPTER FIVE

It is difficult for a person to comprehend a voyage on a sailing ship measured in months and weeks when today, a flight in a modern jet aircraft is timed in hours and minutes spanning the same distance. In the waning years of the 19th century the "Down-Easters" marked the beginning of the end of the wooden sailing vessel, as the steamers with their dependable schedules were taking the cargoes from the square riggers. Many of the sailing vessels continued albeit in lesser numbers. The writers sang their praises and used adjectives like handsome, beautiful, a masterpiece and exceedingly well built, to describe the vessels that had been built in shipyards up and down the coast of Maine. Their names were well known. *Henry B. Hyde, A.G. Ropes, Benjamin F. Packard, James Drummond* and *The State of Maine* were but a few.

One of the prettiest "Down-Easters" was the four masted barque *Shenendoah,* built by the Arthur Sewall Company, in Bath in 1890. Her beauty earned her image a place of honor on all registers and licenses of American ships and masters. Captain Jim Murphy claimed that she sailed like a knock-about sloop. Along with many other of her kind, she was retired after 20 years of circling the globe and she finished her years being towed behind a tug as a lowly barge. She was rammed and sunk off Shinnecock Bay, Long Island, New York on October 20, 1915.

The age of sail was passing, but not yet gone. The final chapter in the history of wooden sailing ships was the big multi-masted schooner. It began in 1880 with the construction of the first four-masted schooner, the *William L. White.* Between 1880 and 1889, sixty-eight of these vessels were built in Maine. In 1888, the first five-masted, the *Gov. Ames,* was built in Waldoboro. Even today, the town claims to have been first. On Route 1, just outside of town a sign reads: Waldoboro, the home of the first five-masted schooner. The *Gov. Ames* measured 1,778 tons and was 245 feet long. It was not immediately successful and more vessels of this rig were not built until the turn of the century. Their cargo was coal. Tons and tons of black diamonds to warm the homes and factories of New England during the long cold winters.

Above: The schooner *Spindrift* on the day of her launching in 1920. She went in the water ready to sail. The vessel left on what was supposed to be a short run across the Bay of Fundy to Halifax and ran into a gale. Soon after that some planking let loose and many other problems developed. It was obvious that the schooner was not as well built as most of her counterparts in Maine. The short run ended up in the Azores where everyone was glad to get on dry land. Records do not show what happened to the schooner after that but her register was abandoned in 1924. *Photo courtesy of the Sullivan-Sorrento Historical Society, Sullivan, Maine.* **Below:** The Maine shipyards built a total of 327 four masted schooners. This is the *Keating* coming down the ways at the I.L. Snow & Co., in 1919 at Rockland. She was of 698 tons and was 184 feet long. After her launching she was renamed *Dorothea L. Brinkmann* before she left on her maiden voyage. She was wrecked just five years later at Oregon Inlet in North Carolina. *Photo courtesy of James Stevens, Boothbay, Maine.*

The three masted schooner *Howard W. Middleton* was sailing through dense fog on August 11, 1897 when she grounded on Higgins Beach in Scarborough. The vessel was hard on the beach at low tide. The crew came to the beach in the ship's boat without injuries. The schooner was out of Philadelphia for Portland with a cargo of coal. Efforts to haul the vessel off the sands failed and she broke up in heavy surf. Her skeleton is still visible today at low tide just off Higgins Beach. *Photo by William P. Quinn.*

On August 4, 1900, the first six-masted schooner came down the ways at Camden. The *George W. Wells* measured 2,970 tons and was 319 feet long. She was followed two months later in Bath by the *Eleanor A. Percy,* 3,400 tons and 323 feet long. The names of the masts were: fore, main, mizzen, jigger, driver and spanker. There was a total of nine of these huge wooden vessels built in Maine between 1900 and 1909. They could carry an enormous cargo of coal, between 5,000 and 6,000 tons each. There were some problems with the big fore and afters. Many were quite heavy in the bow and a little less so in the stern. This tended to make them hog terribly and after a few years they leaked constantly.

Some sharp views were expressed by many mariners about the big schooners. Captain Charles A. Drew, a tug master from Portsmouth, New Hampshire said: "They are as limber as a snake, built of hoop poles and caulked with eel grass."[1] They leaked, they hogged and many were wrecked along the coastline. They did however, make big money for their owners. Passage from the mid-Atlantic coal ports to New England averaged between five and twenty days. When the steam cargo vessel began to dominate the coastal trades, the schooners continued to sail but their numbers dwindled in the 1920's. Fewer were sailing in the 1930's and a rare few in the 1940's. In the end, the vessels were laid up in almost every port along the east coast. Their hulls settled in the mud, their masts toppled over and in a few years they were gone.

[1] "The Great Coal Schooners of New England 1870-1909" by Capt. W.J.L. Parker, U.S.C.G. (Ret.).

The large schooners carried huge cargoes. Everything about these ships was enormous. The old adage that the bigger they are, the harder they fall was curiously displayed when the only two six-masted schooners in the world were in a collision. It was a freak accident that occurred at 10:15 p.m. on June 29, 1901, five miles east of Cape Cod. The Bath Daily Times reported that the two ships "tried to sail over the same spot on the vast ocean at the same foggy time with costly results."

The *George W. Wells* had left Boston on the afternoon of the 29th bound for Newport News in ballast. The *Eleanor A. Percy* was bound for Boston loaded with coal. When the accident occurred, the anchor head of the *Percy* caught in the rigging of the *Wells* and then the two giants came together. Captain George Jewitt of the *Percy* said: "Accidents will happen on the best regulated ships. The whole trouble is that we did not see each other in time to get clear, that is all." Captain Arthur Crowley of the *Wells* said: "We had a head wind, The *Percy* had a fair wind. Further comment I do not care to make."

The two vessels were taken to the Percy & Small shipyard in Bath for repairs. The shipyard report outlined the work done on the two ships: New deck beams and decking, new hanging knees, ceilings, waterways and lock strakes. Decks caulked, a new mizzen mast and new mainsail. Everything renewed or replaced that was carried away by the collision. The *Wells* is in new and good order and condition. The *Percy* was fitted with a new jibboom and bowsprit with new planking, new bobstay plates and two new catheads. Both ships returned to sea in first class condition.

On June 29, 1901, the six masted schooner *George W. Wells* was in a collision with the six master schooner *Eleanor A. Percy* five miles east of Cape Cod. This view on deck of the *Wells* shows the damage near the mizzen mast. Forward on deck is the anchor head of the *Percy* imbedded in the deck timbers. *Photo courtesy of the Maine Maritime Museum, Bath, Maine.*

Above: A large section of the port side of the *George W. Wells* was replaced at the Percy & Small shipyard at Bath. The repairs took about six weeks to complete and cost over $20,000. **Below:** The *Eleanor A. Percy* moored at the Percy & Small shipyard at Bath in July, 1901 minus her jibboom and bowsprit. *Photos courtesy of the Maine Maritime Museum at Bath, Maine.*

The custom of breaking a bottle of wine on the bow to launch a ship is said to bring good luck to the vessel but the state of Maine was a leader in the temperance movement. Neal Dow was known as the "Father of Prohibition." He was the author of the "Maine Law" passed in 1851 and Maine was the first state to ban the sale of alcoholic beverages. This lasted until the repeal of National Prohibition in 1934. The lack of liquor sometimes precluded the age old practice of launching a ship off the ways by breaking the traditional bottle of champagne. Some vessels went into the water with flowers, or pure white pigeons, and others with young ladies in white gowns dancing around on deck to bless the ship and send her down to the sea. Other reports show that a few were launched with Maine's famous Poland Spring Water.

They launched the five masted schooner *Arthur Seitz* in 1901 with flowers. Everything went fine until the vessel started to move. The cradle slid sideways and hung there. She had to be blocked up and re-aligned before they could get her in the water. The old salts claimed the lack of wine on the bow jinxed her from the start. She only sailed for one year and was wrecked on Skiff Island Reef near Muskegat Island, Massachusetts in dense fog on May 25, 1902.

Another one of these strange launchings occurred in Brewer on May 5, 1905. The four masted schooner *Augusta W. Snow* was launched at the yard of E. and I.K. Stetson. As she slid down the ways, a young lady released a pure white carrier pigeon. The bird circled around in the air for a few moments and then flew down river bearing a message for persons in Boston. The schooner did not seem to suffer from any bad luck and sailed successfully for thirty years.

In any Maine shipyard, a large crew of men spent between six and nine months constructing one of these large schooners. Launch day was usually one of celebration. Most always, a keg of rum was on hand, Neal Dow notwithstanding, and a few ounces were used to wet down the bow of the vessel and the rest was consumed in the usual manner.

The five masted schooner *Gardner G. Deering* was launched at Bath in April 1903. She was of 1,982 tons and sailed until the late 1920's. The vessel was owned by the G.G. Deering Co., of Bath and was grounded off Brooksville in Eggemoggin Reach in early 1930. On July 4th of that year she was set afire and then sunk. The hull lies in 30 feet of water, parallel to shore and is a location for divers to explore an old schooner wreck in the summer months. *Photo courtesy of Capt. W.J. Parker, U.S.C.G. (Ret.).*

Above: The big five masted schooner *Arthur Seitz* suffered an accident before she was launched in 1901. On launch day the cradle slipped sideways off the launching ways. The slip gave her a list to starboard and most probably scared the people in the launch party on board. The vessel had to be blocked up and the ways realigned to get her in the water. *Photo courtesy of Capt. W.J.L. Parker, U.S.C.G. (Ret.).* **Below:** On May 25, 1902 the *Arthur Seitz* was wrecked on Skiff Island Reef and her wreckage washed up on Tuckernuck Island near Nantucket, Massachusetts. *Photo from the marine collection of Frank E. Claes, Orland, Maine.*

Above: Another large schooner with a short life was the *Helen J. Seitz* launched in Camden in 1905 and stranded at Beach Haven, New Jersey on February 9, 1907. *Photo from the marine collection of Frank E. Claes, Orland, Maine.* **Below:** The auxiliary schooner *David Cohen* was built in 1918 in Dennysville, Maine. Compare this photograph with the launch picture above. The horses and buggies have been replaced by motor vehicles of an early vintage. The vessel was renamed *Victoria S.* in 1921 and she foundered off Ocracoke Beach, North Carolina on August 23, 1925. *Photo courtesy of Wilhelmina Youngquist, Worcester, Massachusetts.*

Above: A dangerous hazard of ice houses was fire. The Smalls ice house on the Kennebec River was ignited by sparks from the power plant while loading a schooner on June 8, 1900. The ice house burned to the ground leaving a huge pile of ice. The schooner escaped without damage.
Below: On June 29, 1910, sparks from a railroad locomotive ignited dry grass and the fire spread to the Haynes and DeWitt ice houses at Iceboro on the west shore of the Kennebec River. Two four masted schooners, the *Young Brothers* and the *Henry L. Peckham* were being loaded at the dock. Sparks set their sails on fire and soon both vessels were engulfed in flames. The ice houses and one of the schooners were total losses. The *Henry L. Peckham* was rebuilt. *Photos courtesy of the Maine Maritime Museum, Bath, Maine.*

Above: A sign of the times in the 1930's. Old schooners were left rotting in the back harbors with the tides running in and out of their holds. Five vessels lay in the mud at Mill Cove at Boothbay Harbor. *Photo courtesy of Bill Fuller, Jr.* **Below:** The four masted schooner *Edna M. McKnight* was launched in Camden in 1918. She worked for nine years and then ended up at Mill Cove in Boothbay Harbor. Her hulk has laid rotting away since 1927. *Photo by William P. Quinn.*

Above: The schooner *Mary Weaver* ran on a ledge in the Sheepscot River in 1919 and the 53 year old vessel was too far gone to save. She was patched and then towed to Boothbay Harbor and beached at Mill Cove. The salvagers stripped her and laid her hull bare on the beach. Some of her keel is still visible at low tide. **Below:** The five masted schooner *Mary H. Diebold* was built in 1920 in Newcastle, Maine and sailed the coastal trade until she was laid up at Broad Cove in Eastport in 1932. In the summer of 1937, she was broken up for her lumber. Her stern cabin was removed and made into a summer cottage. *Photos courtesy of Bob Beattie.*

Above: The four masted schooner *Mary Bradford Peirce* was launched in 1919 at Boothbay by the Atlantic Coast Company. She was a handsome vessel of 1,133 gross tons and she lasted twelve years in the trade. *Photo from the collection of Roger Peterson, Cape Elizabeth, Maine.* **Below:** On July 16, 1931, the schooner *Mary Bradford Peirce* went aground in thick fog on Cape Smoky, sixty miles north of Sydney, Nova Scotia. The vessel was underway in ballast from Eastport for Campbellton, N.B. to load a cargo of wood lath for New York City. The crew reached shore safely but the schooner was a total wreck. *Photo courtesy of Capt. W.J.L. Parker, U.S.C.G. (Ret.).*

Above: The six masted schooner *Wyoming* was built in Bath in 1909 and was of 3,730 gross tons and was 329 feet long. She was the largest wooden sailing vessel to carry a cargo. Her loss in 1924 is still one of the classic unsolved mysteries. She was anchored in gale winds near the Pollock Rip lightship when she went to pieces. Parts of her wreckage and her quarterboard washed ashore on the north side of Nantucket Island. She was fully loaded at the time of her loss and there were no survivors. *Photo courtesy of the Mariners Museum, Newport News, Virginia.* **Below:** The *Cora F. Cressy* was launched in Bath in 1902 and sailed for over 25 years in the coal trade. She ended her days as a breakwater for a lobster pound in Medomak. When this photograph was made in 1975, she was still there. *Photo by Lt. H.M. Dillian, U.S.C.G.*

59

Above: In 1932, the four masted schooners *Hesper* and *Luther Little* were hauled into Wiscasset, Maine, and laid up alongside a wharf. They have never moved since that time and have become a top tourist attraction as they rot away in the elements. *Photo courtesy of Bill Fuller, Jr.* **Left:** This sign has been erected on one of the poles beside the railroad tracks at Wiscasset overlooking the old schooners lying in the mud on the Sheepscot River. **Below:** In 1982 only three masts are standing on the *Luther Little* and the deterioration is gaining on the old hulls. Soon they will be like their sister ships, things of the past. *Photos by William P. Quinn, Plane Piloted by Hank Dempsey.*

Above: The hulls of two of Maine's four masted schooners lie forgotten off Long Island in Casco Bay. The *Maude M. Morey* was built in 1917 by the G.G. Deering Company in Bath, and was of 1,364 tons. The *Zebedee E. Cliff* was built in 1920 by the East Coast Ship Company in Boothbay and was of 1,361 tons. The two vessels were purchased by the Government in 1942 for use as a breakwater. They were later burned and just the lower portion of the hulks remain today. *Aerial photo by William P. Quinn, Plane piloted by Hank Dempsey.* **Below:** A familiar scene in Maine in the early 1900's was a tug towing a group of schooners up river to load at an inland port with lumber or ice. The number of vessels varied from two to as many as five at once. *Drawing by Paul C. Morris, Nantucket, Massachusetts.*

Above: On March 7, 1910, the steamer *Manhattan* of the Maine Steamship Company arrived at Portland from New York. Soon after the vessel was made fast to the pier a fire of unknown origin erupted in one of the forward compartments. Flames spread quickly and the steamer was pulled away from the dock by a tug and was beached clear of other shipping. The ship was a total loss and was sold for scrap. One man lost his life in the fire. The steamer was built in 1891 with a wooden hull of 1,892 tons and was 240 feet long. *Photo from the collection of Roger Peterson, Cape Elizabeth, Maine.* **Below:** Early in the morning on May 25, 1910, the steamer *Belfast* was steaming in thick fog approaching her pier in Rockland when she rammed the steamer *J.T. Morse* a few feet forward of the pilothouse. The *Morse* sank as all of her passengers were being removed. The salvage tug *Orion* of Boston patched and pumped her out and towed her to Boston for repairs. She was off her run for about a month. *Photograph courtesy of the Steamship Historical Society of America, Baltimore, Maryland.*

CHAPTER SIX

A Portland newspaper, "The Daily Argus," carried a column of items for all those interested in maritime commerce. "Happenings on the shore and at sea" It contained comments about the weather, marine news and views, gossip and wreck reports. On August 10, 1911, the following items appeared: "The fresh southwest wind which sprung up yesterday morning blew out to sea the dense fog which has veiled the coast since last Saturday, and all interested in shipping are hoping that the worst of the dog day fogs is over for the season."

"Capt. Charles H. How of this city, who is in command of the *Isles of Shoals* steamer this season, reports a narrow escape from collision with a huge whale on Tuesday of this week when about three miles out from Portsmouth light. The boat was proceeding in a dense fog when Capt. How discovered something dead ahead which looked to him like a big piece of wreckage. A quick turn at the wheel changed the steamer's course, when it was discovered that a big whale was floundering in the swell right in their path. On approach of the steamer it churned up the sea, made several dives and then disappeared to reappear some distance away. Whales have been showing up along the coast this season in unusual numbers, about every steamer coming from New York reporting seeing them off Boon Island and passengers are disappointed if they fail to put in an appearance."

"Steamer *North Land* brought 400 passengers from New York yesterday, the baggage coming with them being enormous. The *Governor Dingley* from Boston for St. John, N.B., also brought a large number of passengers."

"No vessel has actually been reported missing in this vicinity since the gale of Friday, July 28, but it is very evident that some lumber laden vessel must have come to grief in that storm. Several times during the past week wreckage has been sighted by incoming vessels, the last one to so report being the schooner *Sawyer Brothers,* which arrived here yesterday from Perth Amboy. Her captain reports: this side of Cape Cod, passed through considerable quantities of lumber and wreckage, including part of the after house of a vessel."

A significant deficiency was discovered in the big schooners on November 6, 1911, when the five masted schooner *Samuel J. Groucher* ran aground on a ledge off the Isles of Shoals. She ran up on a high tide and the weather was calm but the vessel had 4,000 tons of coal aboard and when the tide went out, so did the coal. The schooner's hull split wide open and she was a total loss.

On January 10, 1912, the 2,241 ton steamer *Carolyn* of New York ran up on the rocks at the northeast end of Metinic Island at the southwest entrance to Penobscot Bay. The ship had a crew of 27 and a cargo of paper and potatoes. Vessel and cargo valued at $400,000 were a total loss. Life Savers from the White Head Life Saving Station went to the wreck in their surfboat and assisted the crew in transferring personal belongings to the cutter *Androscoggin*. The steamer later broke up on the rocks.

Above: The two masted schooner *Tay* with lumber from St. John, N.B., to Boston, ran into a heavy southeast gale on the night of July 27, 1911. She was off Bar Harbor when the mainsail parted and the main boom cracked. **Below:** The vessel was too close to shore to work off under head sails and was dashed on the beach. One man was lost when the schooner was wrecked on Sand Beach. *Photos courtesy of the Bar Harbor Historical Society, Bar Harbor, Maine.*

Above: The schooner *Fannie & Fay* ran aground at Kennebunkport while going out the river on August 8, 1911. The vessel was lying easy and was refloated on the 11th. She was bound for Stonington but was forced back in the river by a strong easterly wind. *Photo courtesy of Frank E. Claes, Orland, Maine.* **Below:** During the first ten days of August in 1911 the coast of Maine was covered by dense fog. The Bath Daily Times reported that several narrow escapes from collision had occurred. On August 7th the schooner *Eleazer Boynton,* laden with gravel, was anchored in the harbor at Rockland. She was struck by the steamer *Camden* and she sank immediately. The crewmen were rescued but the schooner was a total loss. *Photo courtesy of the Steamship Historical Society of America Photo Bank, Baltimore, Maryland.*

As long as men have sailed ships on the sea, one shipwreck stands out, above all others, as the greatest in history. That one was the *Titanic*. On April 14, 1912, the brand new White Star liner was steaming along in the North Atlantic at 22½ knots on her maiden voyage to America. Just before midnight, the big four stacker was pierced by an iceberg. Her location was at 41-46 North and 50-14 West, or about 400 miles southeast of Newfoundland. The iceberg tore a huge 300-foot long underwater gash in the side of the vessel. The ship had 14 lifeboats, 2 cutters and 4 collapsible boats with a total capacity of 1,178 persons, or, a little more than half of the 2,223 aboard. At this time, there were no international maritime laws governing the number of lifeboats on ocean liners. Besides, the *Titanic* was supposed to be unsinkable. This illusion of safety prevailed until the inevitable was realized. Unfortunately, 467 lifeboat spaces had left the ship unfilled.

The cream of European and American society was on board along with eleven millionaires including John Jacob Astor and Benjamin Guggenheim. These men went down with the ship. At 2:10 a.m. the huge ship sank, a little over two hours after she struck the iceberg. There were 1,517 persons lost, and only 706 people survived in lifeboats. Thirteen ships had heard the SOS and were speeding through ice filled waters to the scene. The *Carpathia* was first to arrive at 3:30 a.m., she picked up all of the survivors and carried them to New York City. The aftermath of the disaster resulted in demands for strict regulations for ocean liners.

The White Star Liner *Titanic* leaving on her maiden voyage in Europe. The vessel was of 46,328 tons and was 882.6 feet long with a beam of 92.6 feet. Her value of $7,500,000. She departed Queenstown, Ireland on April 11. 1912. *Photo courtesy of the Titanic Historical Society, Inc., Indian Orchard, Massachusetts.*

A serious lifeboat shortage ensued when liners in ports all over the world tried to bring up the number of their lifeboats to the capacity of passengers on board. Following the *Titanic* disaster, the Marconi Company was unable to provide all of the radio operators for the ships that now needed them. New schools were opened to train more wireless men.

Since the disaster, many books have been written about that memorable night. Immediately following the sinking, the International Ice Patrol was established in the North Atlantic. At that time, two United States cutters alternately scouted the Grand Banks area and reported to ships by radio the drift of all icebergs in the vicinity of the transatlantic steamship lanes. Each nation using the northern steamer routes paid its share of the expense. The modern patrol today uses aircraft and each year they mark the anniversary of the sinking of the *Titanic*. A Coast Guard aircraft flies to the position, 400 miles southeast of Newfoundland and drops a ceremonial wreath, hoping that it will come to rest near the gravesite of the *Titanic* two miles below the surface. The wreath is donated by the Titanic Historical Society. The trip is a little more than ceremonial, as the crew searches for icebergs during the entire flight.

The United States Life Saving Service annual report for the fiscal year ending June 30, 1912 reported: "Although the loss of the steamship *Titanic* did not occur within the scope of the Life-Saving Service, it is deemed not inappropriate to present in a report dealing largely with statistics of marine disasters a few facts relating to a vessel that was, during her brief career, the largest ship ever built, and to set forth some of the important events associated with her untimely destruction. Nothing can better assist one to comprehend the vastness of this, the most appalling maritime tragedy of the age, than the statement that the number of persons who perished when the steamer went down exceeded by nearly 200 the total number of persons lost within the field of the Life Saving Establishment since its organization—a period of more than 40 years."

The two masted schooner *William Rice* had laid over in Boothbay Harbor to escape bad weather off shore. She was bound from Boston to Thomaston with a cargo of ten tons of cement. The vessel raised sail on November 7, 1912. Later that morning, she was blown ashore on Ocean Point at the southern tip of Linekin Neck at Boothbay. The storm completely wrecked the schooner which was built in 1869 at Bath. The crew of three was saved as was the cargo of cement. *Photo from the collection of Roger Peterson, Cape Elizabeth, Maine.*

Above: The Maine Central steamboat *Norumbega* aground at Clarks Point near Northeast Harbor on August 13, 1912. This was a very peculiar accident. Firemen had banked the fires anticipating a short run across the harbor. A delay in her departure caused the vessel to run out of steam halfway to her destination and she grounded in dense fog on a high tide. *Photo courtesy of Allie Ryan, South Brooksville, Maine.* **Below:** When the tide dropped the steamer lay on her starboard side. She was later pulled off with little damage. *Photo courtesy of Bob Beattie, Belfast, Maine.*

The wooden sailing vessels were slowly being replaced by steamers with dependable schedules. On May 31, 1913 the collier *F.J. Lisman* grounded on Squaw Point about five miles below Bangor on the Penobscot River. She lay on a sand bar over a tide and was pulled off without damage. The *F.J. Lisman* was of 2,294 tons, 247 feet long and her steam plant generated 1,300 h.p. *Photo courtesy of Steve Lang, Owls Head, Maine.*

A little more than two years after the *Titanic* disaster, the liner *Empress of Ireland* was in a collision with the Norwegian collier *Storstad* in dense fog in the St. Lawrence River. The accident occurred at about 2 a.m., on May 29, 1914, off Father Point near Rimouski, Canada, about 80 miles north of the state of Maine. The tragedy took the lives of 1,024 people. The ship was struck amidships in the boiler rooms and was immediately plunged into darkness. The vessel sank in only fourteen minutes which would account for the high death toll. Many passengers were thrown into the cold water and were lost. Lifeboats from the collier were launched to pick up survivors from the liner. The deaths of over a thousand persons in this wreck did not command the headlines that surrounded the *Titanic* disaster. More passengers were killed in this accident than either the *Titanic* or the sinking of the *Lusitania* in May, 1915. These were everyday people and the *Empress of Ireland* was a small steamer with none of the elite personages aboard. This would explain somewhat the lack of importance attended with the disaster.

The *Empress of Ireland*, 14,000 tons, 550 feet long. On May 28, 1914 the liner was rammed by the Norwegian coal freighter *Storstad* in dense fog. The ship sank in the St. Lawrence River in 150 feet of water. 1,024 persons were lost in the accident. *Photo courtesy of the Peabody Museum of Salem, Salem, Massachusetts.*

Above: The German liner *Kronprinzessin Cecilie* laying in Bar Harbor on August 4, 1914 after her run across the Atlantic to escape capture. The liner remained in Bar Harbor for two months and then was taken by the United States and later used as a troop transport in World War I. *Photo courtesy of the Bar Harbor Historical Society, Bar Harbor, Maine.* **Below:** The Maine Central Steamer *Norumbega,* pulled alongside the *Kronprinzessin Cecilie* and transferred her passengers and their baggage ashore. *Photo courtesy of the Steamship Historical Society of America.*

On July 28, 1914, World War I began in Europe. A week later, persons in Bar Harbor woke up to find the German liner *Kronprinzessin Cecilie* in the harbor. There were 1,216 passengers and thirteen million in gold on board. Her Captain, Charles Pollak, fearful of losing his vessel to the enemy, steamed back across the Atlantic following the declaration of war between Germany and England. The Maine Central Railroad steamer *Norumbega* transferred the passengers to shore where they departed by train. The treasure was carried to shore by the Revenue Cutter *Androscoggin*. The *Kronprinzessin Cecilie* lay in Bar Harbor until November, when she left under the escort of a cutter and two destroyers and sailed to Boston. The crew was interred and the liner was overhauled. She was renamed the *U.S.S. Mount Vernon*. She became a troop transport and carried more than 35,000 American soldiers to Europe after the United States entered the war in 1917.

THE LOSS OF THE ALMA E.A. HOLMES

On October 10, 1914, the steamer *Belfast,* sailing from Bangor to Boston in dense fog was in collision with the four masted schooner *Alma E.A. Holmes* off Bakers Island in Massachusetts Bay. Captain Frank Brown of the *Belfast* held his vessel's bow in the gaping hole in the schooner's side for ten minutes, giving the crew of nine an opportunity to leave the vessel. After all hands were safe, the steamer backed out and the schooner filled and went down in twenty fathoms of water. The *Belfast* had 150 passengers on board who witnessed the rescue. Captain Henry A. Smith of the *Holmes* said that there was little warning of the collision and his loss was great as he had been master of the vessel for sixteen years. The schooner, together with the personal property of the crewmen was a total loss. The *Alma E.A. Holmes* was built in 1896 in Camden by Holly M. Bean and was of 1,208 tons. She was on a voyage from Norfolk, Virginia to Salem, Mass. with 1,819 tons of coal.

The war in Europe had a direct effect on Maine shipping. The Bath bark *William P. Frye* was stopped by a German Raider in the South Atlantic on January 27, 1915. The ship was loaded with wheat bound for Queenstown. The Germans took provisions and removed the crew. They set dynamite charges and sank the ship. The bark was built in 1901, was of 3,374 tons and had a crew of 32. She was sunk at Lat. 29-45N, Long. 24-50W. *Photo courtesy of Maine Maritime Museum, Bath, Maine.*

The annual report of the Revenue Cutter service for 1914 described the cutter *Woodbury* as the oldest vessel actively employed by the U.S. Government. "She was built in 1864 in Philadelphia, and is 146½ feet long and displaces 500 tons. The cutter is now over 50 years old and has reached a stage where due to her rotting timbers and leaky boiler it is difficult to keep her in proper condition for cruising. In spite of her weaknesses she manages to patrol the coast of Maine from Portland to Eastport." At that time, a new cutter was being considered for the station and in August, 1915, the *Woodbury* was retired and replaced by the cutter *Ossipee*.

On January 13, 1914, the old cutter *Woodbury* was anchored in fog in Penobscot Bay. Early in the afternoon she received a radio message to go to the aid of the steamer *Cobequid,* aground on Trinity Ledge, Nova Scotia. The old cutter steamed across the Bay of Fundy in heavy seas with temperatures below zero and she iced up badly. The cutter arrived at the scene of the wreck on the morning of the 15th and found that the seventy passengers had been saved by others and the steamer was a total wreck. The cutter returned to U.S. waters and was immediately directed to Matinicus Rock lighthouse where the schooner *Northland* was in need of assistance. The schooner had a frostbitten crew of 12 and a cargo of 2,046 tons of coal aboard. Her sails had all been blown out, booms and gaffs broken, a jury tiller rigged and she was leaking badly. The cutter *Woodbury* towed her into Rockland Harbor.

For 40 years, along the coastline of the United States where crews of the Life Saving Service and the Revenue Cutter Service were cooperating in rescue work, there was, unavoidably, some duplication of effort, results and reports. In 1915, there was a major change in the two services. They were combined into one unit on January 28, 1915, and became the United States Coast Guard. The combining of the two services was a natural move as better co-ordination between shore and sea units resulted in a higher degree of efficiency in operations of the life saving field. At that time, the equipment of the Coast Guard consisted of 24 cruising cutters, 18 harbor cutters and 279 shore stations. Duties were to continue as before, except that in time of war, the Coast Guard operated as part of the Navy, subject to the orders of the Secretary of the Navy.

Operations of the Coast Guard during World War I followed the laws set down earlier by Congress. A wartime incident occurred off the coast of Maine when surfmen from the White Head lifeboat station had to deliver a message to the steamer *City of Bangor* warning her to return to port because of the danger of submarines. There were 99 persons aboard the steamer on June 10, 1918 when the message was delivered. One tragedy marred the war effort of the Coast Guard. The cutter *Tampa* was torpedoed on the night of September 26, 1918 in the Bristol Channel, England. She was lost with her entire complement of 112 men. Six Coast Guard cutters were employed in convoy and escort duty in European waters, the *Ossipee, Seneca, Yamacraw, Algonquin, Manning* and *Tampa* forming a part of the U.S. forces based on Gibraltar, which escorted hundreds of vessels between the Mediterranean and Great Britain.

The crew of the White Head Life Saving Station situated on an island at the entrance to Penobscot Bay. The boat ramp with rollers made for easy launch and recovery of the surfboat in all kinds of weather. *Photo courtesy of Richard M. Boonisar, Norwell, Massachusetts.*

Above: An early morning fog caused the collision between the steamers *Pemaquid* and *J.T. Morse* on September 8, 1915, at the western entrance to Deer Island thoroughfare near Stonington, Maine. Captain Addison W. Shute managed to bring his vessel into a wharf on Moose Island before it sank to her freight deck. Passengers and cargo were removed and the ship made tight and pumped out. She then went to Boston under her own power for repairs. *Photo courtesy of the Steamship Historical Society of America.* **Below:** The schooner *Lanie Cobb* stranded on the ledges in front of the West Quoddy Head light in dense fog on September 17, 1915. She carried a cargo of coal for Calais, her home port. Life Savers assisted crewmen in saving property from the vessel which was a total loss. The schooner was built in 1874 in Brewer, Maine. *Photo courtesy of Roger Peterson, Cape Elizabeth, Maine.*

Above: The three masted schooner *William L. Elkins* was caught on a reef off Cape Elizabeth, Maine during a northeast gale on December 6, 1915. The vessel was out of Calais and had a cargo of fish. The Coast Guard cutter *Ossipee* arrived on the scene and removed the crew of six along with their personal belongings. The schooner was a total loss. **Below:** A serious fire aboard the *SS Herman Winter* caused her to be towed out of Portland harbor to the south shore and beached on March 14, 1916. Fire boats pumped so much water into the after hold that she sank and rested on the soft bottom mud. Wreckers removed much of her damaged cargo and refloated her on March 26th. She was then towed to Boston and underwent repairs in a drydock. *Photos courtesy of Robert Beattie, Belfast, Maine.*

The steamer *Bay State* ran aground at Cape Elizabeth in dense fog on September 23, 1916. *Photo from the collection of W.H. Ballard.*

The steamer *Bay State* was a sister ship to the *Portland*. The *Portland* was lost in November 1898 in the great gale that bears her name. The *Bay State* remained in port that night and continued to sail between Boston and Portland until 1916. She was built in Bath in 1895 and was of 2,262 tons and was 281 feet long. Her engines generated 1,200 horsepower. She was an elegant steamer and was on the run for over twenty years. On September 23rd while making her approach to Portland Harbor in dense fog the vessel went up on Holycomb Ledge off Cape Elizabeth. The cutter *Ossipee* was dispatched to her aid and surfmen from the Cape Elizabeth station arrived and transferred passengers from the steamer to the cutter and other vessels standing by. They took off fourteen of her crew by breeches buoy. After the passengers were removed, their baggage and the ship's cargo were unloaded by a small fleet of harbor craft. There were plans to salvage the steamship but late October storms broke the hull open and she was a total loss.

A wartime measure with lingering effects was the Volstead Act, or Prohibition. In January 1919, the necessary thirty-six states had approved the 18th ammendment to the United States Constitution and the rest of the nation joined Maine's teetotallers in a provisory ban on liquor. Times changed rapidly and prohibition brought on the speakeasy, the bootleggers, the rum-runners and the roaring twenties.

Above: The steamer *Bay State* lies on Holycomb Ledge with extensive hull damage. **Below:** Late October storms broke up the steamer and she was a total loss. *Photos courtesy of the Peabody Museum of Salem, Salem, Massachusetts.*

Above: The two masted schooner *Willis & Guy* ran ashore on the ledges of Pemaquid Point in dense fog on August 15, 1917. Captain John S. Lowe and the crew of four reached shore in the ship's boat. The schooner had a cargo of 215 tons of anthracite, out of Port Reading for Halifax. The vessel was built in 1873 in Belfast and was of 199 tons. **Below:** The pounding seas broke the 40-year-old hull into pieces and it was a total loss. *Photos courtesy of the Fisherman's Museum at Pemaquid Point, Maine.*

Above: The Gloucester fishing schooner *Elizabeth Howard* was bound for Portugal in the fall of 1917 with a cargo of dried fish. The vessel was anchored in East Boothbay harbor while her crew was ashore. She grounded on a low tide and lay over on her side. When the tide came in it flooded over her hatches. **Below:** The salvage vessel *Sophia* righted the schooner and pumped her out. The cargo of fish was taken to Boothbay Harbor and dried out again and then reloaded aboard the schooner. The vessel then sailed to Portugal and delivered her cargo intact. *Photos courtesy of James Stevens, Boothbay, Maine.*

Above: On Monday, August 26, 1918, the small steamboat *Tourist* was approaching the dock at Damariscotta when a crankshaft pin broke on the engine. The vessel lost headway and swung broadside in the river. The current carried her down river under a bridge where she capsized and sank. Passengers and crew were spilled into the water and many swam to shore while others were picked up by small boats. One man was drowned in the mishap. The steamer was raised and rebuilt. She was renamed the *Sabino* and continued to steam in the Maine waters. *Photo courtesy of Frank E. Claes, Orland, Maines.* **Below:** After a series of owners the vessel was acquired by the Mystic Seaport Museum in Connecticut in 1973 and is one of the few remaining coal-fired passenger steamers still working in the United States. Summer cruises are offered on the Mystic River. *Photo by Kenneth E. Mahler, Mystic Seaport.*

The two masted schooner *Herman F. Kimball* went ashore stern first at Long Point on Cape Elizabeth in dense fog on September 5, 1918. The vessel had a cargo of 96,000 feet of lumber from Windsor, N.S. for Boston. Life Savers removed the crew by breeches buoy and later most of the cargo was saved but the schooner went to pieces on the rocks. The vessel was of 125 tons and was built in 1888 in Boothbay Maine. *Photo courtesy of Roger Peterson, Cape Elizabeth, Maine.*

Above: The five masted schooner *Carroll A. Deering* on the day she was launched at Bath, Maine, April 4, 1919. *Photo courtesy of the Maine Maritime Museum at Bath.* **Below:** The *Charles H. Trickey* on the left and the *Mary E. Olys* both hit ledges at the entrance to Cape Porpoise on the stormy night of January 1, 1920. The vessels were both lost. *Photo courtesy of Capt. W.J.L. Parker, U.S.C.G. (Ret.).*

CHAPTER SEVEN

The sea has a strange fascination to man. The oceans have countless mysteries: phantom ships, the Flying Dutchman, Davy Jones' locker and the enigma of the *Marie Celeste*. A lesser known puzzle is the ghost schooner from Bath, Maine. The five masted *Carroll A. Deering* was launched at Bath on April 4, 1919, and was of 2,114 tons. The schooner was returning to Portland from Rio de Janeiro in ballast and made a stop at Barbados, British West Indies and then set sail for Norfolk, Virginia. On January 29, 1921, the schooner passed the Lookout Shoals Lightship off Cape Hatteras, North Carolina. A storm blew up after that and the next time the vessel was seen was on the 31st when she was spotted at dawn by a surfman on beach patrol. She had all sails set and was hard aground on Diamond Shoals. The seas were mountainous when the surfmen rowed out to the wreck. They could not get close enough to go aboard because of the heavy swells. There were no signs of life aboard and the heavy seas were washing over the schooner.

Four days later, the ocean flattened down somewhat and the surfmen went aboard the stranded vessel. At this time, the mystery deepened. In the cabin, food was on the table with a fire going in the stove. There were no signs of foul play. The ghost schooner had been abandoned by all except the cat; a mute witness. No trace of the crew or the yawl boat has ever been found. No one has any knowledge of what went on during the last time the vessel was seen by the lightship and when she was found wrecked on the shoals. Was it mutiny, piracy or murder? One theory was that the ship was attacked by rum runners. Many other ideas were put forward. The crew could have been washed overboard in the storm. No distress signals were ever sent out from the schooner. No evidence has ever been found to substantiate any theory.

Investigations into the incident were held by the Navy, Coast Guard, and The Treasury, State, Commerce and Navigation Departments. The official Government report in the annual List of Merchant Vessels stated that the ship was lost by stranding on Cape Hatteras with the loss of eleven men. The families of the crew suspected foul play was involved. There are many unanswered questions in the evidence that is known. Later the vessel broke up and her pieces washed ashore. Today the skeleton of the ghost schooner is buried in the sands of Ocracoke Island on the outer banks of Cape Hatteras, North Carolina. A grim reminder of a mystery that only the dead crew can answer.

The Atlantic Coast Pilot lists Cape Porpoise Harbor as "midway between Portsmouth and Portland and is often a welcome haven for cruising craft caught in a blow on this stretch of coast." On January 1, 1920, the three masted schooner *Charles H. Trickey* was caught in a blowing snowstorm off the Maine coast. She was out of Portland for Lynn, Massachusetts with a cargo of boxboards. Cape Porpoise has a very narrow channel with ledges on either side. When the schooner entered at midnight, she piled up on one of the ledges. Six hours later, another Captain had the same idea. The three masted schooner *Mary E. Olys* out of Stonington for New York with a cargo of granite headed for safe anchorage out of the storm. Her captain didn't know about the wreck of the *Charles H. Trickey*. At the last moment, through almost zero visibility, he saw the wreck and veered off but it was too late and the helpless vessel piled up on another ledge. The plight of the schooners was soon discovered and the cutter *Ossipee* was dispatched from Portland to assist. There was nothing the cutter could do to save the grounded vessels. They were soon turned over to the wreckers. The cargoes from both schooners were saved but the hulls pounded to pieces and were a total loss.

A good example of Murphy's Law occurred in 1920 at the Adams Shipyard in East Boothbay. The motor vessel *Seaward* was launched with two cradles under her keel. One cradle became fouled and the hull slid out and tipped over. Her 96 tons smashed the whole side of the building as she lay down and came to rest, a far distance from floating. *Photo courtesy of James Stevens, Boothbay, Maine.*

Above: While the yacht *Seaward* lay on her side, the men at the shipyard dug under the capsized hull and built a cradle and ways and then unceremoniously launched her into the water. As she entered the water, the hull popped upright and floated on an even keel. *Photo courtesy of James Stevens, Boothbay, Maine.* **Below:** An example of the popularity of the steamship in Maine waters is illustrated in this photograph of the *Ransom B. Fuller* loading passengers at the Popham Wharf for a Sunday excursion in 1903. The steamer was built in 1902 for the Bath to Boston run and she was of 1,862 tons. *Photo by James E. Perkins, courtesy of Jane Stevens, Bath, Maine.*

Above: The concrete steamer *Polias* was wrecked in Penobscot Bay on Old Cilley Ledge off Port Clyde in a blizzard on the night of February 6, 1920. Eleven of her crew were lost when they set out in a lifeboat during the worst of the storm. The following day, the Coast Guard cutter *Acushnet* saved the remaining 27 crewmen and brought them to Rockland. **Below:** The decaying concrete hull lay on the ledge and deteriorated to a grotesque form in the middle of the bay. Some say that the ghosts of the lost crewmen haunted the hull until she finally slipped under the water. *Photos courtesy of the Maine Maritime Museum, Bath, Maine.*

Above: Some of the old schooners remained at sea too long. The two masted schooner *Robert W.* was built in 1847 and was in the trades until January 12, 1923. She was carrying a load of box boards from Thomaston to Lynn, Mass. when she was caught in a northeast gale. The schooner was having a bad time in the storm when she hit York Beach. She lay on her beam ends on the outer bar with her crew of two men lashed in the rigging. After the tide dropped, rescuers brought the frost bitten men ashore and revived them. The vessel was a total loss. *Photo courtesy of the Kittery Marine Museum, Kittery, Maine.* **Below:** In the winter of 1922-23 the U.S. Coast Guard cutter *Ossipee* smashed her way through the ice on the Penobscot River near Bangor. It was necessary to keep the waterway clear in order to avoid ice jams which would lead to serious flooding. The cutter made good progress breaking the ice which was between ten and fourteen inches thick.

THE WANDBY

The old adage "to err is human" might have the common ending: Sometimes it's very expensive! A costly accident occurred on March 9, 1921, when the British tramp steamer *Wandby* piled up on the rocks at Walkers Point in Kennebunkport in dense fog. The steamer was of 3,981 tons, in ballast, out of Algiers for Portland, Maine. Her master claimed he mistook the Kennebunk River for the Kennebec River. While headed for Portland? The Coast Guard sent a boat out to the vessel from the Biddeford Pool station but the crew was in no danger and remained on board to assist in salvage. The investigation revealed that the steamer hit the rocks at her normal cruising speed. This left the bow high up on the point. The cutter *Ossipee* arrived on the scene but could not get close enough to the grounded freighter because of the shoal water. The ship had holes in her hull from the grounding. Water was rising inside the vessel with the tide. On March 11th, the crew was removed and taken to Portland for transportation home on the next ship to England. For weeks the *Wandby* lay on the point and was an attraction for hundreds of townspeople and others visiting from surrounding areas. Wreckers were called in and the vessel was cut up for scrap.

The steamer *Wandby* aground at Walkers Point off Kennebunkport. Coast Guard surfmen in the white boat maintained a watch on the grounded freighter. *Photo by Whitcomb Studio, courtesy of the Brick Store Museum, Kennebunkport, Maine.*

Above: The tide went out and the *Wandby* lay stranded on the rocks. *Photo by the Whitcomb Studio, Kennebunkport, Maine.* **Below:** The remains of the steamer *Wandby* as salvage crews cut up the hull for scrap metal. *Photo courtesy of the Brick Store Museum, Kennebunkport, Maine.*

Above: The steamer *City of Rockland* had a career marked by frequent accidents including collisions with other Maine steamers. The mishap that finished the vessel occurred on September 2, 1923 when she piled up on the ledge off Dix Island at the mouth of the Kennebec River. After she lay on the ledges for several days, the Merritt Chapman Company refloated her and towed the steamer to Boston. *Photo courtesy of Paul C. Morris, Nantucket, Massachusetts.* **Below:** The steamer *City of Rockland* down by the stern on the ledges of Dix Island. After she was refloated, a survey found it impractical to restore the vessel and she was sold to the wreckers. *Photo courtesy of James Stevens, Boothbay Harbor, Maine.*

THE CITY OF ROCKLAND

The steamer *City of Rockland* was of 1,696 tons, 274 feet long and had a 1,600 H.P. engine. She was launched in Boston in 1900 and was the epitome of elegance. She could carry 2,000 passengers as well as 600 tons of freight but the ship was accident prone. Mishaps among Maine steamers were not uncommon but not usually habitual. In her 23 years, the *City of Rockland* had more than her share. The first notable accident occurred on July 26, 1904, when the steamer struck a ledge in Muscle Ridge Channel in dense fog. After they floated her off, she had to return to Boston to be rebuilt. (See page 42.) Two years later, in June 1906, the *City of Rockland* was rammed by her sister ship, the *City of Bangor* in dense fog off Portland. The *Bangor* hit the *Rockland* aft of the after gangway and swept everything above the guard into the rooms for about 15 feet. On April 26, 1910, the steamer ran aground at the entrance to the Kennebec River in thick fog. Surfmen from the Hunniwells Beach Life Saving Station assisted in getting the steamer off and underway again. In 1912, the vessel was in another collision in dense fog with the collier *William Chisholm* about 30 miles east of Boon Island. Another collision occurred in 1913 with the schooner *H.P. Havens.*

Her later years were marred by frequent disasters and on the night of September 23, 1923, she was wrecked on Dix Island at the mouth of the Kennebec. The steamer had left Bath and was on her way to Boston in dense fog. At 7:30 p.m. there was a crash as the boat struck and then slid up on the ledge. Distress signals were sounded with the ship's whistle. Before long, the Coast Guard boarded her and removed the 350 passengers as the steamer settled by the stern. The passengers were returned to Bath where they boarded a train to Boston. At low tide, the steamer made a spectacular picture as she was balanced on her keel on the rocks. There was a huge hole in her bow. After the vessel was hauled off the ledge, she was towed to Boston. A survey of the hull showed that it was impractical to restore her to service. The *City of Rockland* was taken to Salem, Massachusetts where she was stripped of all usable fittings and lumber and then the hull was burned on Little Misery Island.

The steamer *City of Rockland* sunk at a pier in Boston in 1924 prior to her stripping and burning at Salem. *Photo courtesy of Robert Beattie, Belfast, Maine.*

Above: On January 26, 1924, the steamer *Gov. Bodwell* ran up on Spindle Ledge near Swan's Island in a blinding snowstorm. Distress signals brought out the island fishermen who removed the passengers and mail. The vessel was later salvaged and rebuilt. She went back on the run for a few more years. *Photo courtesy of Frank E. Claes, Orland, Maine.* **Below:** The *Truro Queen*, 386 tons, was built at Economy, Nova Scotia in 1918. She was lost on a voyage from Norwalk, Connecticut to St. George, N.B. when she ran ashore in dense fog at Egg Rock, off Jonesport, Maine on July 10, 1924 and became a total loss. *Photo from the collection of Paul Sherman, Hudson, New Hampshire.*

92

Above: A ship aground is a curiosity that attracts sightseers wherever it happens. The *J.T. Morse* steamed in Maine waters from 1904 to 1931 and experienced a few accidents along the way. She was struck in 1910 in Rockland and sunk. She was in another bad collision in 1915 and on July 23, 1924 in dense fog, went up on a ledge off Crotch Island. **Below:** The vessel was pulled free on the next tide with little damage. *Photos from the Ballard Collection, courtesy of Maine Maritime Museum, Bath, Maine.*

Herbert Hoover dubbed it "The Noble Experiment." When prohibition began in 1919, smuggling was immediately in vogue. The underworld realized the tremendous profits involved in contraband liquor. It wasn't long before "Rum Row" was set up. A line of Canadian fishing vessels loaded with whiskey, positioned just outside the three mile limit. They sold liquor to rum runners in fast boats that outran the coast Guard patrol boats near shore. It was an embarassing situation for the Coast Guard and for three years, they could not meet the challenge.

Funds were voted by Congress in 1923 for newer and faster vessels to capture rum runners. They transferred twenty destroyers from the Navy to the Coast Guard. Thirteen million dollars was voted for new construction and a new twelve mile limit was enacted into law. With the new equipment, the Coast Guard was able to hold their own against the smugglers. Many were arrested and had their boats confiscated to be used against other boot-leggers, but for every one caught, a dozen more escaped. Those brought into court would find lienient juries, secretly fearful for cutting off the supply. Following the trial, rum runners were back on the high seas again the next night.

The islands of St. Pierre & Miquelon served as a warehouse for the illicit liquor trade. The "Rum Row" vessels would load up and head south to trade along the Atlantic coastline. John Greenleaf Whittier wrote: "O Hundred Harbored Maine" in his poem about the Dead Ship of Harpswell—There were probably more than a hundred deserted coves along Maine's coast that the smugglers could slip into on foggy or moonless nights and land the illegal liquids.

The old schooners never seemed to die. The *Mary Langdon* was built in Thomaston in 1845 and was a typical freighting schooner. The vessel was repaired, rebuilt and restored down through the years and in 1925 was anchored a couple of miles east of Nobska Lighthouse off Cape Cod with a load of lumber piled high on deck. The Coast Guard became suspicious and asked her Captain to move out of the island steamer lane. When the Skipper refused, the schooner was arrested and unloaded. An intensive search under the lumber turned up 2,000 cases of scotch whisky. The camouflage did not fool the Coast Guard and the vessel was seized and sold at auction. She did not last long after the sale. *Photo courtesy of Mariners Museum, Newport News, Virginia.*

Above: The shallow draft vessel was the typical "Rum Runner." Long, sleek and fast, able to carry enough cargo to be profitable but not too much to slow the boat down to risk capture. *Photo courtesy of the Smithsonian Institution, Washington, D.C.* **Below:** The fishing vessel *Shamrock* was entering Linekin Bay near Boothbay Harbor on July 15, 1924 and misread the buoys. She was headed for Dick Tibbets ice house to ice up for a fishing trip when she went up on Spruce Point ledges. She heeled over at low tide but was pulled off without damage on the high tide. The vessel proceeded on her fishing trip on July 15th. *Photo courtesy of the Peabody Museum of Salem.*

There are many rocks and reefs that skirt the entrance to Portland Harbor. One of the most dangerous is Trundy's Reef situated between Cape Elizabeth and Portland Head. On November 21, 1920, the aging schooner *Pochasset* was battling a northeast gale, trying to work into the shelter of Portland Harbor. The vessel approached Cape Elizabeth and when she tried to come about, lost her way and struck on the ledges of Trundy's Reef. The crew attempted to launch the yawl boat but it was fouled and the gasoline engine could not be started. The crew sought shelter in the damaged forward cabin as the wind pushed the seas higher. The waves continued to smash the stranded schooner as the crew huddled, wet to the skin, praying that their vessel would hold together and weather the storm. Early the next morning, the vessel was spotted. Within minutes the Coast Guard brought out a large power boat to the scene. The seas were still high, and with much difficulty the crew of the schooner was rescued and brought to shore. The *Pochasset* broke up that evening and her lumber cargo was strewn out all along Cape Elizabeth and was salvaged by the local residents.

Many vessels came to grief on Trundy's Reef. The shoal extends out about a mile from the Cape and was the scene of several wrecks. Two years after the *Pochasset,* a large collier went up on Trundy's Reef and lay there for almost two weeks. Early in the afternoon of May 18, 1922, the big steamer *Middlesex,* laden with 7,600 tons of coal was entering Casco Bay in dense fog. The steamer was moving at moderate speed. With no warning, she ran up on Trundy's Reef. The tide was rising at the time and it was believed that she would float off at high water. The cutter *Ossipee* and two Portland tugs arrived and tried to pull the steamer off the rocks but could not move her. The forward half of the vessel lay on the reef while the stern was afloat. Rocks had penetrated the hull and the forward hold was flooded. The cargo of coal had to be off-loaded before the ship could be refloated. Time was of the essence as a storm would break up the vessel. More than half the cargo was taken from the forward holds and on May 30th the collier was floated off the reef. The holes in her hull were patched and she then steamed to Boston where repairs were completed in a dry dock.

In December 1926, the three masted schooner *Emily F. Northam* stranded on the mud flats off Big Cranberry Island after breaking her moorings at Islesboro. The mountains of Mount Desert Island can be seen in the background. *Photo courtesy of Farnham W. Smith, Carlisle, Massachusetts.*

The three masted schooner *Emily F. Northam* was wrecked on Baker Island Reef, south of Mount Desert Island on December 2, 1926. The vessel was lying easy and was not badly damaged. The Coast Guard removed the crew and brought them to the Little Cranberry Island station. A few days later, a salvage tug pulled the schooner off the reef and grounded her at Islesford. Another storm hit the area and the vessel went adrift across Islesford Harbor and ended up on the mudflats on Big Cranberry Island. Workers managed to remove the cargo of lumber and loaded it aboard the lighter *Ajax*. The lumber was sold in Rockland and the hull of the schooner rotted on the mud flats.

Above: Workmen unloading the lumber cargo from the hold of the schooner *Emily F. Northam* after the schooner grounded on the mud flats of Big Cranberry Island. **Below:** The lighter *Ajax* loading the lumber cargo of the *Emily F. Northam*. The entire cargo was recovered from the grounded schooner. *Photos courtesy of Farnham W. Smith, Carlisle, Massachusetts.*

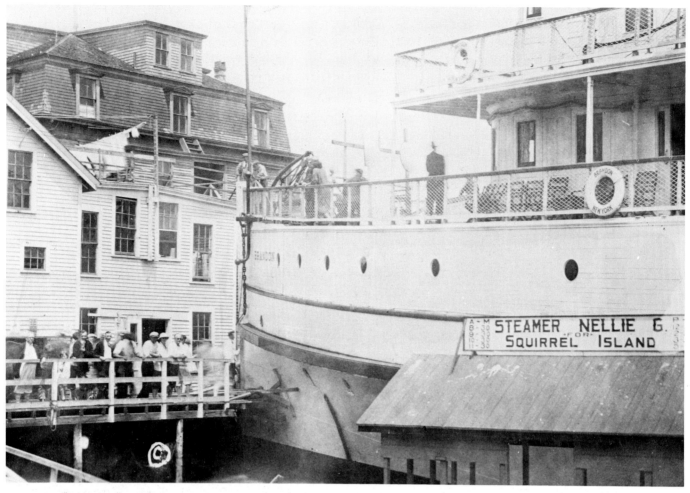

Above: On July 11, 1927, the steamer *Brandon* made a poor landing and rammed her bow about ten feet into the wharf at Boothbay Harbor. A mix up in bell signals was given as the cause of the accident. The vessel was arriving from Boston and although there were many people on the pier at the time, no one was hurt. *Photo from the collection of Roger Peterson, Cape Elizabeth, Maine.* **Below:** The three masted schooner *William Booth* was docked at Vinalhaven on January 26, 1928 when she was torn away from the pier by a gale and cast ashore. The damage was slight and she was refloated on February 6th and towed to Rockland. The schooner met a violent end on May 7, 1928 when she was in collision with the four masted schooner *Helen Barnet Gring* off Chatham, Massachusetts and was lost. *Photo courtesy of Capt. W.J.L. Parker, U.S.C.G. (Ret.).*

Above: The schooner *Camilla May Page* grounded on the rocks at Jefferey's Point at the entrance to Portsmouth, New Hampshire harbor on November 18, 1928. The vessel had a full load of coal on board and was leaking badly. A couple of weeks later, storm seas destroyed the schooner after only 15 tons of coal had been removed. *Photo from the collection of Paul C. Morris, Nantucket, Massachusetts.* **Below:** The three masted schooner *Wawenock* with a load of granite, from Sullivan, Maine to New York encountered a storm offshore and tried to find shelter near Isle au Haut. She struck Brimstone Ledge in the fog on January 11, 1929. She was abandoned by her crew. The vessel then floated off the ledge and came ashore on McGlathery's Island. The cargo was removed and the vessel was a total loss. *Photo courtesy of Capt. W.J.L. Parker, U.S.C.G. (Ret.).*

Above: The Casco Bay steamer *Pilgrim* was running in thick fog on July 6, 1929 when she stranded on a rocky ledge on Deer Point at Great Chebeaque Island. The vessel was ashore 11 hours before the Coast Guard cutter *Chicopee* pulled her off. The steamer was towed back to Portland by the steamer *Emita* and had to be repaired in a drydock. *Photo courtesy of U.S. Coast Guard.* **Below:** The Army tug *General R.N. Batchelder* went up on a ledge in Whitehead Pass, Cape Elizabeth in dense fog on September 10, 1929. 20 passengers were taken ashore by the steamer *Maquoit*. The tug was hung on the ledge until October 3rd when the cutters *Chicopee* and *Tuscarora* refloated her. *Photo courtesy of U.S. Coast Guard.*

Above: The four masted schooner *Dorothy* was built in 1896 at Bath as the *Goodwin Stoddard*. She was registered in Eastport in 1929 where the vessel was abandoned. In the photo, she was run up on the beach and stripped. *Photo from the collection of Roger Peterson, Cape Elizabeth, Maine.* **Below:** The ferry *Hockomock* was a familiar landmark in Bath. She was nicknamed the Hunky-Dink. The vessel was built in Bath in 1901 and plied the Kennebec between Bath and Woolwich until the opening of the Carleton Bridge in 1927. She ended up on the mud flats in South Portland where she was abandoned. *Photo— Allie Ryan Collection, Maine Maritime Academy.*

Above: The fishing vessel *Lochinvar* piled up on a submerged reef off Portland Head Light in thick fog on October 4, 1932. The accident occurred shortly after 6 p.m. and crewmen immediately went into the schooner's dories. A few minutes later the vessel rolled off into deep water and sank. The schooner had about 20,000 pounds of fish in her hold. A Maine photographer made this spectacular photograph using the light from the lighthouse to illuminate the scene. The vessel broke up in the next storm and was a total loss. *Photo from the marine collection of Frank E. Claes, Orland, Maine.*

Prohibition had a debilitating effect on society. The period between 1920 and 1930 was labeled the lawless decade. The underworld controlled the liquor business all over the United States. Smuggling spawned other types of crime that spread corruption from law officers to the courts and politicians. Gangsters became rich as prohibition created chaos all over the country. Problems, however, sometimes find a way to correct themselves. In October 1929, the stock market crashed and brought a decline in business and employment. A deep economic depression followed and the United States Treasury receipts dwindled. There were many arguments presented for repeal of prohibition. One was the fact that liquor could be taxed to help the country's financial woes and reduce the crime rate somewhat. It wasn't the panacea for financial recovery but every little bit helped. In November 1933, the 21st amendment was ratified and prohibition was repealed. Thus ended a formidable chapter in Coast Guard history. The service waged a difficult and unpopular battle against smugglers. They had less than 300 vessels to patrol a coastline of over 5,000 miles. About one patrol craft for every 300 square miles of ocean. However, in the 14 years that prohibition was law, personnel carried out their duties and maintained the high standards of the Coast Guard.

A veteran steamer went down at the dock due to old age. After nearly fifty years steaming on Penobscot Bay, the *Vinalhaven* sank at her pier in Rockland in November 1938. She was raised, and the metal parts sold for scrap. The wooden hull was cast away to rot on Monroe Island Bar in the Muscle Ridge Channel. *Photo from the marine collection of Frank E. Claes, Orland, Maine.*

CHAPTER EIGHT

The decline of the coastal passenger steamer began soon after the end of World War I. Automobiles were being manufactured in greater numbers. More than eight million were in use across the country in 1920. Competition from trucks took away much of the freight from the steamers. The trucks and cars were a faster mode of transportation along new roads that enabled people to travel where and when they wanted without resorting to schedules. By 1930, only two overnight passenger steamers were still on line: the Boston-Bangor steamers *Camden* and *Belfast* of the Eastern Steamship Line. On December 27, 1935, the last run west was made by the *Belfast*.

The Boston-Bangor line had been established in 1823. The first vessel was the side wheel auxiliary steamer *Bangor*, 160 feet long and of 400 gross tons. It required 25 cords of wood to fire the boilers for the trip from Boston to Bangor. At the pinnacle of steam travel, vessels used to ply regularly from Boston and New York to all ports in Maine, year round. Steamers that left Boston for the Maritime Provinces used to call at Portland, Boothbay Harbor, Rockland, Bar Harbor, Jonesport, Lubec and Eastport.

There were some true-blue steamboat enthusiasts who mourned the passing of these classic steamers. Many books were written extolling the beauty of Maine Steamboats. One of the more interesting was "Steamboat Lore of the Penobscot" by John M. Richardson, published in 1941, which was still being reprinted 30 years later. The book was extensively illustrated with multiple photographs and a descriptive history of each vessel. Mr. Richardson followed each steamboat from its launch to the final run on the line, and then to the demise of the vessels. The book is an authoritative narrative on the Maine steamboat.

Above: The Eastern Steamship Lines' freighter *Sagamore*, 2,599 tons, with a crew of 26 headed out of Portland, Maine, at midnight on January 14, 1934. She was bound for New York in a northeast blizzard, with promises of improving weather. The freighter later ran up on Corwin's Rock four miles off shore as her look-outs could not spot Willard Rock light buoy, which was out at the time. The hull was leaking badly, and it was decided to beach the vessel. She came ashore on a reef off Prouts Neck. The Coast Guard sent a boat out the next morning to remove her crew. The cargo was salvaged but the ship was a total loss. *Photo from the Ballard Collection by Ralph Blood.* **Below:** The 10,000 ton steamer *Iroquois* ran up on Bald Porcupine Island at Bar Harbor in dense fog at 3:30 a.m. on July 12, 1936. The ship was underway for New York City at the time. Her steel bow was almost up in the trees. After daylight, 144 passengers were taken off and had to make the trip to New York by train. That afternoon, after a hole in the bow was sealed with plank and timber, the ship was pulled off on the high tide by the U.S. Minesweeper *Owl*. Repairs were made later in New York City and the steamer returned to Bar Harbor on July 24th. *Photo courtesy of the Steamship Historical Society of America.*

Above: The Norwegian steamship *Kings County* ran up the rocks near Lornville, New Brunswick in darkness, fog and rain on December 10, 1936. The wind and a strong tide drew the vessel off her course. One member of the crew became a hero when he swam through the mountainous seas 100 feet to the cliff and shore with a rope which he tied to a large boulder. The crew then made the rope fast on the mast and went ashore hand over hand on the life line. The ship was a total loss. *Photo by John Lochhead, courtesy of the Mariners Museum, Newport News, Virginia.* **Below:** A steamboat that had her roots in Maine was a victim of the 1938 hurricane that killed 588 persons in southern New England. The *Monhegan* was built in Rockland in 1903 and was on the Portland to Rockland run until 1917. The steamer was sold south and ran in Rhode Island waters until September 21, 1938 when she sank at her slip off Dyer Street in Providence. One of her lifeboats was carried away by the storm and was found in the doorway of a restaurant, four blocks away. She was refloated and taken to Rocky Point Amusement Park to be used as a night club but that failed and she was hauled to Prudence Island where she was abandoned. *Photo by Loren Graham, courtesy of the Steamship Historical Society of America.*

Above: The collier *Berwindvale* was entering the Kennebec River at low water on January 10, 1939 when she struck an uncharted ledge and suffered damage below the water line. The ship was taking water faster than the pumps could handle it so she was beached on the west bank of the river. The Coast Guard cutter *Kickapoo* came down from Bath to assist the steamer. **Below:** The vessel floated off the beach at high tide and with the *Kickapoo* as escort, proceeded up river to Bath to discharge her cargo of 6,700 tons of coal. The steamer went to Boston for repairs. *Photos courtesy of Maine Marine Museum, Bath.*

Above: On August 8, 1939 the Gloucester fishing vessel *Annie & Mary* was lost in fog off the Maine coast. Early in the morning she ran up on the rocky ledges off Richmond Island. The crew of seven men launched a dory and left their vessel. They were picked up by another fishing vessel in the vicinity. The Coast Guard answered distress signals from the *Annie & Mary*, located the shipwrecked crew and brought them ashore. The vessel had grounded at high tide. Salvage attempts were made but the dragger would not move. The vessel was abandoned and was a total loss. *Photo by Gardner Roberts, Portland Press Herald.* **Below:** The rotting skeletons of four wooden vessels lie between Little Diamond and Great Diamond Islands in Casco Bay. The vessels were towed out from Portland Harbor for disposal. Similar hulks are found in many coves and bays up and down the coast of Maine. *Aerial photo by William P. Quinn, Plane piloted by Hank Dempsey.*

On the morning of May 24, 1939, the U.S. Navy submarine *Squalus* sank while on a routine training dive off the coast of New Hampshire. Later that afternoon the sub tender *Falcon* arrived on scene and prepared to send divers down. The rescue bell was carried on the stern. *Photo courtesy of Portland Press Herald.*

THE SQUALUS

On May 24, 1939, just after eight in the morning, the U.S. Navy submarine *Squalus* was on a routine training dive off the Isles of Shoals when a high speed induction valve stuck open flooding the after compartments. The sub went to the bottom, stern first in 260 feet of water. She lost all power and the emergency circuits had shorted out. Fifty-nine men were aboard, 26 in the after flooded section and 33 in the forward compartments. Shortly afterward, communications were set up between the sunken vessel and another submarine on the surface. The Navy rushed the submarine tender *Falcon* to the scene to try to save the 33 men. Divers went down breathing a special mixture of helium and oxygen. They attached a cable to the forward hatch of the sub to guide a diving bell down. The rescuers succeeded in bringing the 33 crewmen to the surface on the next day. The remaining 26 men in the after section had drowned when the sub sank.

The Navy intended to save the submarine. It was new and undamaged. The attempt to raise the sub began at once. On July 13th, the bow shot up out of the water for ten seconds and then sank again to the ocean floor during a mishap in the salvage operations. On September 13th, they brought the sub to the surface and then towed her up the Piscataqua River to the Navy Yard. They discovered 25 bodies in the after compartments. One man was missing and the mystery has never been explained. The Navy spent $1,400,000 to refit the sub and in 1940, she was re-commissioned the *U.S.S. Sailfish* and served in World War II.

Above: The work of rescue began aboard the *Falcon*. A diver was lifted over the side to dive on the sunken submarine. On the left, the diving bell. *Photo courtesy of the National Archives, Washington, D.C.* **Below:** This photograph made on May 25, 1939 shows the diving bell returning to the surface with survivors of the *Squalus* being helped to the deck of the *Falcon*. 33 men were saved by the bell. *Photo courtesy of Portland Press Herald.*

Above: The bow of the *Squalus* raised out of water for ten seconds on an aborted salvage attempt on July 13th. The sub sank again and was not raised for another month. *Photo by James A. Jones, Boston Globe, courtesy of the National Archives, Washington, D.C.* **Below:** The rescue vessel *Falcon* was the support vessel for the salvage of the *Squalus*. The photograph shows ballast being blown out of pontoons attached to the sunken submarine. *Photo courtesy of Portland Press Herald.*

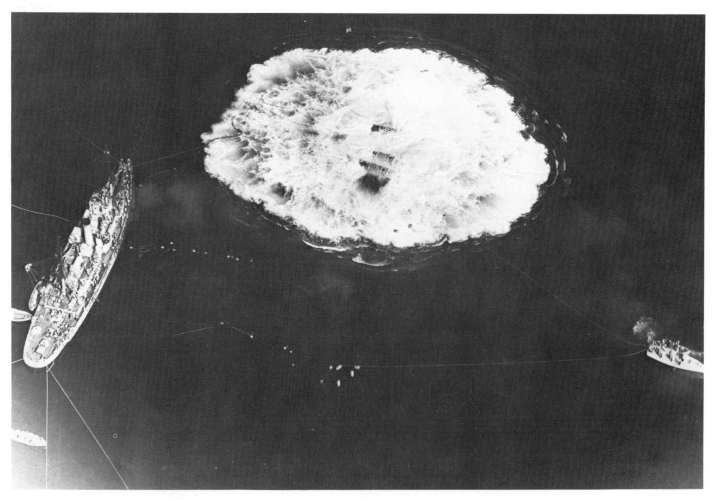

Above: On September 13, 1939 the submarine *Squalus* came to the surface in a successful salvage and was towed to Portsmouth Naval Base for refitting. *Photo courtesy of Portland Press Herald.* **Below:** The conning tower of the *Squalus* serves as a memorial to 26 men who drowned when the submarine sank. The tower was removed and erected on the Navy Base at Kittery. *Photo courtesy of U.S. Navy, Kittery, Maine.*

The tugboat *Seguin,* towing a barge up the Kennebec River on June 18, 1940, hit a submerged pier at the Richmond Bridge holing her on the starboard side leaving a four foot gash. She dropped the barge and headed for the Dresden shore where she was beached with only the forward end out of water. The salvage lighter *Sophia* came down from Rockland, and a diver patched the hole and the lighter pumped her out. She was taken to Portland for permanent repairs and then returned to the Kennebec. The *Seguin* was built in 1884 and is the oldest documented steam vessel in the United States and is currently undergoing restoration at the Percy & Small shipyard in Bath. The work is being carried on by the Maine Maritime Museum and will bring the *Seguin* back to her former operating condition to maintain a planned live exhibit on the Kennebec River. *Photo courtesy of the Peabody Museum of Salem.*

The fishing vessel *Pemaquid* went ashore at Christmas Cove on Monhegan Island in dense fog in the summer of 1941. She landed high on the rocks and the crew was able to step ashore. The vessel was later floated free by the rising tide and towed to her home port. *Photo courtesy of the Fisherman's Museum at Pemaquid Point, Maine.*

CHAPTER NINE

World War II began in Europe on September 1, 1939, when Germany invaded Poland. England and France immediately declared war on Germany. Overseas demands for war goods created a desperate need for ships. Every hull available was put into service. A few of the old Maine schooners that had not rotted away hoisted their sails again. The four masted schooners *Theoline,* built in 1917 in Rockland; the *Herbert L. Rawding,* built at Stockton Springs in 1919 and the *Reine Marie Stewart,* built at Thomaston in 1919 all carried cargoes during the early years of the war. The *Stewart* was a victim of the war. In the summer of 1942, she was sunk off the coast of Africa by a German submarine.

Another tragic submarine accident occurred on June 20, 1941, when the U.S. Navy sub 0-9, sank 24 miles off the coast of Maine in 440 feet of water. Parts of the interior insulation of the submarine were picked up on the surface, which confirmed suspicions that the vessel had collapsed. Divers were sent down to inspect the hull, but they encountered breathing problems at the depth of 370 feet and had to return to the surface. The submarine was given up as lost with her crew of 33 men.

A tragic end to a pleasant outing occurred on Sunday, June 29, 1941, when the 44-foot cabin cruiser *Don* disappeared with all on board. Thirty-six persons from Rumford had chartered the boat for an excursion trip to Monhegan Island. They planned to enjoy a clambake on the island and return that evening. Captain Paul Johnson left West Point at 10:15 a.m. and just after they cleared Small Point, a thick fog rolled in and the *Don* sailed into oblivion. The boat never reached Monhegan Island. A few days later, bodies of the passengers began to wash up on the islands in the lower bay. The first theory was that the boat had exploded and burned but the bodies had no burns and were fully clothed. Others thought that the boat might have struck a submerged ledge and went down fast before life jackets could be donned. The bodies washed ashore on other islands, some as far west as Cape Elizabeth. The answer to the tragic loss of the *Don* and her 37 souls on board has never been found. No conclusive evidence was available but on August 2, 1963, a section of the *Don* was brought up in a fishing drag. The remains were found by two fishermen in the eastern area of Casco Bay near Round Rock. The condition of the wreckage supported the theory that she went down immediately after striking the ledges.

The cost of war is measured in the losses. Hundreds of ships and thousands of men were lost to submarine action in the North Atlantic. The tanker above is on her way to the bottom. Millions of gallons of oil and gas were spilled into the ocean during World War II. *Photo courtesy of the U.S. Coast Guard.*

In December 1941, Pearl Harbor in Hawaii was attacked by air and sea forces of the Empire of Japan. This brought the United States into the world wide conflict. The war news usually dominated the headlines in the newspapers and marine casualties were generally censored. Anyone appearing near the harbors or shorelines with a camera was suspected of spy activities; so few photographs were made except those by official photographers of the armed forces.

On January 8, 1942, the Army mine sweeper *Arnold* was disabled twenty miles off the Isles of Shoals in stormy seas. The mine sweeper *Baird* was towing the *Arnold* back to port when her seams opened up and she sank so quickly none of her ten crewmen escaped. One man survived the tragedy, the Captain of the 98 foot vessel, William A. Chesteen of Waterford, Connecticut, who was picked up by the *Baird* after he was thrown into the ocean from the bridge. The Coast Guard conducted a search of the area but found only empty life belts and overturned lifeboats.

A vigilant coast watch was carried on during the war for an early warning of any submarine activity. The alert personnel maintained a high degree of efficiency. The collier *Oakey L. Alexander* with her small superstructure, closely resembled the silhouette of a submarine, when eight to ten miles off shore. There were numerous instances when the outposts along Maine's beaches would report a sub sighted. Clear heads in command would check the movements of the collier and most always the position would match the sighting report exactly.

There were a couple dozen four stack destroyers built by the Bath Iron Works in the years between 1910 and 1920. The *U.S.S. Buchanan* was launched on January 2, 1919. She was named in honor of the founder of the U.S. Naval Academy. The vessel saw duty in the Atlantic and Pacific, then was laid up and de-activated for a period. When World War II broke out, the *Buchanan* was transferred to the Royal Navy as part of the Lend Lease Pact. The old destroyer served in the British Navy as the *H.M.S. Campbeltown* and in March of 1942, she was destined for a moment of glory.

The ship was chosen to be a floating bomb to cripple the Normandie drydock at St. Nazaire in France. The Germans had planned to use the dock for repairs to their capital ships. The *Campbeltown* was packed with explosives and in a daring night raid, she was rammed into the fifty-foot high gate of the drydock. The huge charge was set off the next morning by a delayed fuse and killed many Germans who were aboard searching to defuse the ship. The results rendered the drydock useless for the duration of the war. The old *Buchanan* was blasted away but her mission had been accomplished. A Maine built ship completed her destiny twenty-three years after her launching at Bath.

On March 27, 1942 the fully loaded Standard Oil tanker *S.S. Maine* was torpedoed by a German U-boat and sank in a smoking inferno off Cape Hatteras, N.C. A Coast Guard pilot from the Elizabeth City air station was patroling the area and guided a destroyer to the scene. Disaster struck so quickly the crew had only time to dive over the side of the tanker. Without boats and rafts, they struggled to evade the flaming oil spreading over the water. Out of four lifeboats only one was found later with six survivors on board. The other lifeboats dropped empty into the oil burning water from burned boat falls. Empty life rafts floated about. Many of the crew were picked up by the destroyer. *Photo courtesy U.S. Coast Guard, Washington, D.C.*

During the war, there were reports of Germans landing spies and saboteurs from submarines along the coastline of the United States. There were three well known landings on the Atlantic coast. One was the Amagansett Landing which occurred in June, 1942 on Long Island. Another in Florida near Jacksonville and the third on Hancock Point in Maine. In all three, the spies failed to carry out their missions because all were spotted by observant Americans and arrested by the authorities. There were rumors during the war that a large force had landed at Popham Beach and there was a shoot-out with Federal Agents and men of the Coast Guard. Witnesses claim to have seen bodies of dead Germans lined up on the beach one morning. There was an incident where many German bodies were lined up on the beach at Popham but it was not from a landing force. Earlier the alert coast watchers had spotted a submarine on the surface near Bailey's Island in Casco Bay. The Navy was notified and soon two destroyers were moving at flank speed toward the sub. Off Cape Small, just west of Seguin Island, the submarine was depth charged and sank. A few days later, the bodies of German sailors washed ashore near Popham and this confirmed the sinking of the submarine.

The German submarines took a heavy toll in ships in the North Atlantic in World War II. On April 16, 1942, a Nazi sub operating in the Atlantic sank the British Merchant ship *Empire Thrush*. A Coast Guard patrol plane made this photograph as the ship went under. *Photo courtesy of U.S. Coast Guard.*

The collier *Hartwelson* was battling heavy seas on March 6, 1943, when she ran up on Bantam Rock, about five miles south of Newagen. The seas pounded the vessel apart on the rocks and she broke in two. The Coast Guard carried out a dangerous rescue of the 38 crewmen aboard the broken steamer. The lifeboats and rafts had been swept away by the mountainous seas. The Coast Guard shot a line aboard the collier and the men were pulled to safety, one by one, over this line. The rescue required four hours to complete and only one man was sent to a hospital suffering the effects of exposure. Six of the crewmen were from Maine.

In World War II, many odd accidents occurred to men in the Navy. Destroyers stationed in the North Atlantic encountered high seas most of the time, and it was rugged duty. In May of 1943, a big wave broke over a destroyer and swept a seaman off the after deck house into the ocean. A life ring was tossed to him by a shipmate, but he was soon lost in the high seas and could not be found. Forty minutes later, he was getting tired and cold when another destroyer came along and the seaman was taken by a big wave and deposited on the new destroyer's fantail—and he lived to tell this tale.

On December 3, 1944, the two masted schooner *William H. Jewell* sank at her pier in Rockland, Maine. The vessel was just seven years short of being 100 years old. The schooner had been a familiar sight on the Penobscot River, carrying lumber between Bangor and Rockland. One of the worst tragedies of the war occurred on April 23, 1945, in the Gulf of Maine about twenty miles off Cape Elizabeth. A 430 ton Navy Patrol boat was torpedoed off shore with the loss of 49 men out of a crew of 62. A destroyer picked up 13 survivors and brought them into Portland. Two weeks later, the war ended in Europe.

Above: The U.S. troop transport ship *Henry R. Mallory* was torpedoed and sunk by a Nazi U-boat early in 1943 in the North Atlantic. The Coast Guard cutter *Bibb* raced to the scene and picked up survivors clinging to life rafts in the storm tossed seas. More than 300 American soldiers, sailors and Marines were lost in the sinking. *This photograph was made by a Coast Guard Combat Photographer on the cutter Bibb.* **Below:** On February 11, 1944, the British steamship *Empire Knight,* 7,244 tons, bound from St. John, N.B. to New York City missed a buoy off the coast of Maine and ran up on Boone Island Ledge. A northeast storm was blowing a gale and the bow of the freighter was hard up on the ledge while the stern was tossed around by the high seas. An SOS was radioed, and Coast Guard and Navy units rushed to the scene. However, on scene, rescue was next to impossible because of the mountainous seas. The next morning, the ship broke in half and the stern section sank almost immediately. Men and boats were tossed into the sea and the final count was 20 saved and 24 lost. Eventually the bow was smashed by the seas and sank. *Photo by the United States Navy, courtesy of the National Archives, Washington, D.C.*

The five masted schooner *Courtney C. Houck* was built in 1913 at Bath. She was of 1,627 tons and was 218 feet long. The schooner worked in the coal trade for eight years. The vessel then took part in a unique experience for a Maine schooner. She starred in the Hollywood film "Cappy Ricks"—a story about a Maine boy from Thomaston who made good. Following her movie career the schooner went back to hauling coal. She was abandoned at Boothbay Harbor in 1940 and lay in the mud for five years. On Aguust 15, 1945, she was set afire to celebrate the end of World War II. *Photo courtesy of Bill Fuller, Jr.*

Peace returned to the world in 1945. In May, Germany surrendered and the guns fell silent in Europe. In August, the United States unleashed a secret weapon to end the war in the Pacific. The atomic bombs destroyed two Japanese cities and most of their inhabitants. Japan surrendered a few days later. The war brought out some valuable inventions for peacetime use. One useful addition was radar. Primarily designed to detect enemy aircraft in wartime, it was adapted to surface ships to enable them to navigate in fog, storms and on dark nights. The electronic eye was a proven aid to navigation and supposedly could eliminate collisions on the high seas. Later developments have placed radar in aircraft for safety in the air and on landings.

The Plimsoll mark is a series of load lines on the sides of ocean going ships indicating the depth to which the vessel can be loaded in different trades relative to prevailing weather in various zones. There is one mark; WNA, especially designed for one area in the world: Winter in the North Atlantic. This ocean is a confusion of weather—like a witch, brewing up gales and storms in a caldron. Storms born off Newfoundland grow from a gale to a full hurricane with nothing in their path but open ocean and vulnerable ships. The winter of 1951-52 seemed to be one continuous storm in the North Atlantic, and scores of ships were broken down at sea; salvage tugs steaming 24-hours a day could not keep up with the incessant demands for their services. There were fatal accidents, collisions, explosions and blinding blizzards. There were more than 100 m.p.h. winds and 70 foot waves.

In the early days, the Life Saving Service closed their stations every summer during the months of June and July. In the 1950's the Coast Guard was doing just the opposite, in that they reactivated stations that had been closed for the winter months, all along the east coast. The summer boating season adds more work to the Coast Guard function and keeps the men busy.

Above: On March 3, 1947, the 5,284 ton collier *Oakey L. Alexander* with 8,200 tons of coal on board was battling gale winds, high seas, and a snow storm outside Portland, Maine, when the seas ripped 150 feet off her bow. Fortunately the 32-man crew was located in the after section of the ship. Captain Raymond Lewis managed to beach the crippled ship on the rocky ledges of Cape Elizabeth. *Photo courtesy of the United States Coast Guard, Washington, D.C.* **Below:** The Coast Guard fired a shot-line to the broken collier *Oakey L. Alexander* and then set up the breeches buoy. The 32 men crew were all brought to shore safely. *Photo by Gardner Roberts, Portland Press Herald, Portland, Maine.*

Above left: The Coast Guard assisted by volunteers bring a crewman ashore in the breeches buoy from the wreck of the *Oakey L. Alexander*. *Photo by Gardner Roberts, Portland Press Herald, Portland, Maine.* **Above right:** A survivor of the *Oakey L. Alexander* landing on the rocky terrain at Cape Elizabeth, Maine. *Photo courtesy of U.S. Coast Guard, Washington, D.C.* **Below:** A rugged crew of men is required to manipulate the lines of the breeches buoy apparatus during a rescue in high winds and surf. All hands were brought ashore by the Coast Guard from the *Oakey L. Alexander* wreck. *Photo courtesy of U.S. Coast Guard, Washington, D.C.*

Above: The Coast Guard cutter *Cowslip* stood by the wreck of the *Oakey L. Alexander* when she went aground off Cape Elizabeth during an easterly gale on the morning of March 3, 1947. *Photo courtesy of U.S. Coast Guard, Washington, D.C.* **Below:** The wreckage of the *Oakey L. Alexander* was battered by the seas following the rescue of her crew on March 3, 1947 at Cape Elizabeth. *Photo courtesy of U.S. Coast Guard, Boston, Massachusetts.*

Above: The *Joseph P. Connolly* burned out and adrift in the North Atlantic on January 12, 1948. A fire of undetermined origin sent the crew over the side into life boats in gale winds and freezing temperatures. Two other ships rescued the crew of 46 from the boats after they spent nine hours on the high seas. Tugs later towed the burned out hulk into port. *Photo courtesy of U.S. Coast Guard, Washington, D.C.* **Below:** The 110-foot tug *D.T. Sheridan,* underway from Philadelphia to Rockland with two coal laden barges ran ashore in dense fog at Lobster Point on Monhegan Island on November 4, 1948. The Coast Guard removed the crew and there were no injuries. *Photo courtesy of Vernon Burton, Monhegan Island.*

Above: The *D.T. Sheridan* was hard aground. When the tide came in the two barges floated clear. The Coast Guard cutter *Snohomish* arrived on scene and took the two barges in tow for Rockland. **Below:** The tug was a total loss and she went to pieces on the rocks at Monhegan Island. *Photos courtesy of Jake Tibbets, Boston, Massachusetts.*

Above: The greatest foe the sailor has is fire. The Gloucester fishing vessel *St. Christopher* caught fire at sea off the Maine coast in May, 1949. The flames could not be controlled so her Captain headed for Monhegan Island. The boat took the ground at Squeaker Cove. The crew launched their dories and rowed around to Monhegan Harbor for help. *Photo courtesy of Clara Burton, Thomaston, Maine.* **Below:** Later, a salvage vessel arrived at the wreck but the fire had gutted the vessel and she was a total loss. *Photo courtesy of Brewster Harding, Portland, Maine.*

Above: The yawl *Cresta* sailing through thick fog went up on Lobster Point on Monhegan Island in June 1957. The six persons aboard sought help from people on the island to refloat the stranded vessel. **Below:** The next morning, seas started to make up and they pounded the hull so badly that she could not be saved. Some items were salvaged but the yacht was a total loss. *Photos courtesy of Clara R. Burton, Thomaston, Maine.*

Above: The *City of New York,* Admiral Richard Byrd's flagship, used on the first Antartic expedition in the 1920's. In the 1940's she was converted to a cargo schooner and sailed out of Nova Scotia. **Below:** On December 30, 1952, the ship went aground off Yarmouth, Nova Scotia, and caught fire. The crew was rescued by a patrol boat. The ship was a total loss. *Photos courtesy of the Mariners Museum, Newport News, Virginia.*

CHAPTER TEN

When a storm makes up and a ship becomes disabled offshore or a tanker runs aground on a ledge or a ship is beached or a crewman needs medical attention or a thousand other types of accidents occur, they call the Coast Guard. Today's Life Savers are equipped with modern apparatus to enable them to carry out rescues that would astonish their predecessors, who patrolled the coasts for endless miles searching for shipwrecks in the thick Maine fogs. The rubber boots and surfboats have been replaced with up-to-date technology and jet age speed. If the *Washington B. Thomas* (page 39) were to be wrecked today, the entire crew could be airlifted off in minutes in a modern helicopter without even getting their feet wet.

Their motto is "Semper Paratus," always ready. Officers and men of the Coast Guard have to be ever alert. There are times when the many duties will manifest themselves involving more than one of the many diverse functions of the service. Their duties include: "enforcement of the laws on the high seas and in coastal and inland waters of the United States and its possessions; enforcement of navigation and neutrality laws and regulations and the oil pollution act; inspection of vessels of the Merchant Marine; search and rescue; issuance of Merchant Marine licenses and documents; investigation of marine casualties and accidents, and suspension and revocation proceedings; destruction of derelicts; operations of aids to navigation, and publication of Light Lists and local notices to Mariners; and operation of ice breaking facilities."[1]

The prevention of smuggling has always been one of the duties of the U.S. Coast Guard since its founding in 1790 as the Revenue Marine. In the 1920's the service again had to wage war on smuggling as the rumrunners ran wild during the fourteen years of prohibition. Today in the 1980's, some of the lessons learned in the rum war are being recalled as the Coast Guard is again battling smugglers. This time the contraband is marijuana and illicit drugs. The cargo is different but the pattern is the same. A boat load of whiskey was once worth a few thousand dollars to the rumrunner but a boat load of "Pot" can be worth up to a million dollars to the criminals.

Expensive luxury yachts, some costing $100,000 or more, are being used in this illegal trade. Some have been caught and confiscated, with tons of the weed on board. There are many secluded coves and inlets along the Maine coast where a yacht can hide. Even if detected by local residents, it might not be suspected because of its aura of opulent respectability. The Coast Guard has arrested many persons who were suspected of smuggling and has seized numerous yachts and boats; but, as with the liquor war, for every one caught, many more escape.

[1]U.S. Coast Pilot

JONESPORT, MAINE. U. S. LIFE SAVING STATION.   F. B. Adams.

Above: The early Life Saving Stations were built close to the water. This was the Great Wass Island station off Jonesport. **Left:** The first station built at Cape Elizabeth. *Photos courtesy of Richard M. Boonisar, Norwell, Massachusetts.* **Below:** The newest small craft used in the Coast Guard is the 41 foot motor lifeboat. Built for speed and durability, the boat has an aluminum hull with a fiberglass superstructure. It is equipped with twin 275 HP diesel engines that drive it at a top speed of 24 knots with a range of 300 miles. The boat carries a crew of 3 and has a capacity of 21 passengers. *Photo courtesy of the U.S. Coast Guard, Boston, Massachusetts.*

Above: A lightship was placed on station five miles southeast of Cape Elizabeth lighthouse on March 7, 1903 and it marked the approach to Portland Harbor. On February 28, 1975, a large unmanned buoy replaced the modern lightship. There is only one lightship left on the east coast, the Nantucket, on the outer shoals at the ship lane leading to New York. *Photo courtesy of the U.S. Coast Guard, Boston, Massachusetts.* **Below:** The Coast Guard base at South Portland with its large pier and support buildings. *Aerial Photo by William P. Quinn, Plane piloted by Hank Depmsey.*

The HH-52A helicopter, dubbed the "Flying Lifeboat," used for all types of rescues and service. *Photo courtesy of U.S. Coast Guard, Boston, Massachusetts.*

In the late 1930's, Igor Sikorsky invented the helicopter and the vertical take-off flying machine has revolutionized life saving by the Coast Guard. Following World War II, there was rapid development in this machine. On April 16, 1981, the fishing trawler *Pamela D.* reported that the vessel was taking on water about seven miles east of Cape Elizabeth. An H-3 Sikorsky helicopter enroute to Rockland was diverted to the scene and dropped a pump to the fishing boat. They stood by as a lifeboat was sent to escort the vessel back to Portland. Shortly after 5 p.m. on the same day, a research airplane was participating in a radar-tracking experiment when it developed engine trouble and crashed in the sea, about twelve miles off Cape Porpoise. Two men aboard the aircraft parachuted into the water. Another H-3 helicopter enroute to its home base on Cape Cod from Portland was diverted to rescue the two men. Ten minutes later the two flyers were picked up and taken to the Portland Medical Center. A Coast Guard spokesman described the rescues as "all in a day's work."

Above: the Sikorsky HH-3F, nicknamed the "Pelican." The versatility of this unique aircraft makes it indispensable in Coast Guard search and rescue operations at sea. With a 700 mile range, computerized navigation, twin turbine propulsion, the HH-3F added a new dimension to air-sea rescue. The photo above was made during a publicity photo mission and is not an actual rescue. *Photo by Lt. H.M. Dillian, U.S. Coast Guard.*
Below: The men of the Coast Guard risk their lives every time they go out. On February 18, 1979, four airmen aboard an HH-3F helicopter were killed when their aircraft crashed into the Atlantic Ocean. The helicopter was on a rescue mission 180 miles southeast of Cape Cod in thick weather. The sea was rough and, at the time of the accident, it was hovering over a fishing vessel to remove an injured crewman. A huge wave struck the nose of the aircraft on the right side and it rolled into the sea. One airman from the helicopter survived. *Photo courtesy of the U.S. Coast Guard.*

Above: The Albatross, HU-16E amphibious aircraft served long in the air arm of the U.S.C.G. This plane, the last amphibian in U.S. Government service, was retired with appropriate ceremonies in March, 1983. *Photo by William P. Quinn.* **Below:** The new "Guardian" HU-25A jet is a modern sophisticated aircraft to replace the Albatross and will fly the search and rescue missions from the Cape Cod Air Station. *Photo by Gordon Caldwell, Hyannis, Massachusetts.*

A welcome sight on the Penobscot River in Bangor is the Coast Guard icebreaker *Snohomish*. From December through March the vessel keeps the vital waterway open to oil tankers to bring fuel oil products to the area. The *Snohomish* has two diesel engines that develop 1,000 h.p. She serves as a search and rescue vessel out of Rockland for the remaining nine months of the year. *Photo by Robert Mitchell, SN, U.S.C.G.*

Above: George Washington ordered the construction of Portland Head Lighthouse in 1787. The light was completed in 1790 and first lighted on January 10, 1791. The tower is 101 feet above water, the light is 200,000 candle power and is visible for 16 miles. *Aerial Photo by William P. Quinn.* **Left:** The lighthouse at Cape Elizabeth. Originally there were two lighthouses at this station, built in 1828. Cast iron towers were erected in the 1870's. The west light was extinguished in 1924 and the single lighthouse serves today. **Below:** Two Maine lighthouses have been pictured on U.S. postage stamps; the Maine statehood stamp featured the light at Cape Elizabeth. A later stamp depicted the Portland Head Light.

Above Left: The candy stripe lighthouse at West Quoddy Head. **Above Right:** The Coast Guard is keeping up with the space age technologies and converting their remote unmanned lighthouses to solar power. The Goose Rocks Light in the Fox Island Thoroughfare began operating on solar power in October 1982, after being overhauled by men from the cutter *White Lupine. Photo by Lt. jg Kent Mack, U.S.C.G.* **Below:** The rock formations at Pemaquid Point Lighthouse are one of the state's beauty spots. The area is treasured by photographers. *Photo by William P. Quinn.*

The U.S. Coast Guard cutter *Duane* has been based in Portland since 1972. Centrally located along the busy waterfront, the vessel now proudly carries her lettering in gold paint, an honor accorded the oldest active vessel in the U.S. Military fleet. The cutter was commissioned in 1936 and served on convoy duty during World War II in the North Atlantic, the Mediterranean Sea and the Caribbean Sea. Her current duty takes her from Portland out along the Atlantic Coast intercepting drug-smuggling vessels. *Aerial photo by William P. Quinn.*

Above: On November 6, 1982 the *Duane* seized the Panamian freighter *Biscayne Freeze* four-hundred miles southeast of Cape Cod along with her cargo of twenty tons of marijuana. The crew of 24 were taken into custody and the vessel was brought to the support center in Boston. **Below Left:** A U.S. Marshall escorting a prisoner off the cutter *Duane* after the arrival at the support center in Boston. *Photo by Arlee Nodden, courtesy of U.S. Coast Guard, Boston, Massachusetts.* **Below Right:** The Captain of the *Duane,* Commander Leonard V. Dorrian relates the details surrounding the capture of the *Biscayne Freeze* in a dockside press conference in Boston. The electronic media was amply represented as shown by the many microphones present. *Photo by Craig Wellman, Courtesy of U.S. Coast Guard, Boston, Massachusetts.*

The Marshall Point Lighthouse at Port Clyde. The Coast Guard station is no longer used. *Photo by William P. Quinn.*

At the present time, in the 1980's, the Coast Guard maintains numerous cutters and search and rescue (S. & R.) stations along the coast of Maine to protect mariners. There is an S. & R. station at Portsmouth, N.H. At Portland are the large Coast Guard base and the cutters *Duane, Cape Morgan, Yankton, Spar* and *Shackle.* There is an S. & R. station at Boothbay Harbor and at Rockland. Also at Rockland are the cutters *Snohomish, White Lupine* and *Swivel.* Another base is at Southwest Harbor along with the cutter *Bridle.* At Jonesport there is an S. & R. station and the cutter *Point Hannon,* and at Eastport there is an S. & R. station.

Among the many duties relegated to the Coast Guard is the operation of the aids to navigation. Along the Maine coast there are hundreds of buoys, fog-horns, daybeacons and ranges. There are between 65 and 70 lighthouses along the coast and up in the rivers and bays. The reason for the ambiguous number is that some are considered lighthouses and some are not, depending on whether or not they are still working and still used. The scenery around the Maine Lighthouses is picture postcard perfect in most instances. Two of Maine's lights have appeared on U.S. postage stamps, Portland Head and Cape Elizabeth. Some of the old lighthouses are on the list of the Maine State Historic Preservation Commission to become National Landmarks. One of these is Baker Island Light Station off Mt. Desert Island.

At Port Clyde, the Marshall Point Lighthouse has recently been named a public park by local residents. The lighthouse was automated in 1980. The town maintains the park and it is open during the daylight hours. The view across the channel from the light is spectacular. Visible is Hooper's Island and Burnt Island, and on a clear day, one can see all the way to Monhegan. A drive down Route 131 from Thomaston to Port Clyde and from there to the end of Marshall Point Road will bring you to the park.

CHAPTER ELEVEN

America entered the space age in the 1960's. The innovations were almost unlimited. New containerized cargo ships made most other methods of shipping freight obsolete. In 1958, a new rescue program for ships on the North Atlantic was instituted by the U.S. Coast Guard. Initial efforts were successful and in the 1960's the operations were expanded to include other ocean areas, and, finally, the coverage became worldwide. Dubbed the AMVER system, the letters stand for Automated Mutual Assistance Vessel Rescue. It is a merchant vessel plotting program, designed to maintain and provide information on ships for use in "search and rescue" operations. The system is able to forecast the locations of those merchant vessels near an emergency. The computer is told where help is needed and in only moments can identify the names and whereabouts of nearby ships. The rescue center controller handling the case can use this information to radio a suitable vessel on the high seas. Severe storms are tracked and warnings issued based on weather data from ships at sea by satellite reports. The modern computer has made life at sea much safer.

An important AMVER case occurred on April 24, 1969, in the middle of the Atlantic, when a 24 year old crewman aboard the *MV Tielrode* was stricken with an acute case of appendicitis. The German passenger ship *Bremen,* 159 miles away, was the only ship in the vicinity with a doctor on board. The New York Rescue Coordination Center was apprised of the emergency, and they radioed the master of the *Bremen,* who immediately changed course and proceeded to a rendezvous point. The next day, the man was transferred to the *Bremen,* was operated on successfully, and recovered fully. A message from New York to the *Bremen* master: "Your prompt and willing assistance in the emergency medical case was in keeping with the highest tradition of the sea."

The Atlantic Coast Pilot contains a myriad of information for mariners. The information offered on wrecks warns the seamen of the danger areas along the Maine Coast: "Wrecks.—An examination of the record of wrecks along the coast of Maine eastward of Portland shows that wrecks have occurred on practically all of the off-lying islands and rocks between Portland and Machias Bay, most of them in thick weather, either fog or snow. Many of the wrecks could have been prevented if frequent soundings had been taken, or due allowance had been made for the tidal currents setting into or out of bays or rivers.

"During thick weather great caution is necessary when approaching the coast, especially eastward of Petit Manan Island, where the tidal currents have considerable velocity. If one of the offshore lights has not been made and the position accurately determined before the fog shuts in, it would be advisable to keep well outside until it clears. Between Machias Bay and Seguin Island a landfall will be made in clear weather before the outlying dangers are encountered.

"Between Portland and Boston the most dangerous points for coasting vessels are the dangers off Cape Elizabeth, Boon Island, Isles of Shoals and Cape Ann. South of Portland the wrecks have occurred most frequently on the prominent headlands or the shoals off them, namely Cape Elizabeth, Cape Ann and the north side of Cape Cod with less frequent wrecks on the less prominent headlands.

"The inland waters, particularly those from St. Croix River to the vicinity of Portland, contain numerous lobster pots. Small pointed wooden buoys of various designs and colors, secured by small lines, float on the surface; in some cases a second buoy, usually is an unpainted bottle and hard to see, is attached to the lobster pot. These buoys extend from the shore out to, and in many cases across, the sailing routes. Small yachts and motorboats are cautioned against fouling, which is liable to result in a sprung shaft or propeller.

"Fish havens are reefs, constructed by dumping junk; old trolly cars, barges and automobile bodies along a depth curve. Fish havens are outlined and labeled on the charts but navigators should be cautious about passing over or anchoring in their vicinity."

Above: The fishing trawler *Andarte* was swept up on the ledges of Ram Island in Casco Bay in a storm on February 19, 1960. Five crewmen from the trawler were rescued by the Coast Guard at the height of the storm and were landed at the South Portland Coast Guard base by a 36 ' motor lifeboat from the Cape Elizabeth station. The 76 ' *Andarte* was of 93 tons and was built in 1944 at Waldoboro. She was returning to her home port at Portland when she was wrecked. The boat was a total loss. *Photo by Gardner Roberts, Portland Press Herald, Portland, Maine.* **Below:** The 441 foot freighter *Marine Merchant* broke in half just forward of the bridge while battling mountainous seas in a northeast storm in the Gulf of Maine on April 14, 1961. The crew abandoned the vessel early in the morning and were picked up by other merchant ships answering the SOS. The freighter sank at about 10 a.m. Cause of the accident was attributed to improper loading of a bulk sulphur cargo. *Photo courtesy of the U.S. Coast Guard, Washington, D.C.*

Above: On March 19, 1963, the final chapter in a ninety year saga of the sea was written eighty miles south of Cape Sable, Nova Scotia, when the noted Coast Guard cutter *Bear* sank. The ship, while under the Coast Guard, had worked the Bering Sea and Arctic waters for almost thirty years and had rescued hundreds of men. She has seen two eras of ships, sail and steam and was rigged for both. She also served Admiral Richard E. Byrd in 1933 on his second Antarctic expedition. Built as a three masted barkentine in 1873, with an auxiliary steam engine, she had an illustrious career. Famous for her polar exploits, her future was to have been as a historic museum and restaurant in Philadelphia. She was being towed there when heavy weather parted her towline and the foremast collapsed, and then the seas claimed her. Slowly she slipped under the North Atlantic to her last station. *Photo courtesy of the U.S. Coast Guard, Washington, D.C.* **Below:** On November 25, 1963, the Liberian tanker *Northern Gulf* was headed into Portland, Maine, harbor with 261,429 barrels of crude oil when it hit the West Cod Ledge Rock. Twenty-five thousand barrels of oil spilled, polluting the Maine coastline. Damage to the ship was estimated at more than $250,000.00. Cause of the accident was laid to a buoy 400 yards off position. Liability claims were carried all the way to the U.S. Supreme court. The court found for the ship owners and the Federal Government had to pay damages because the buoy was off station. *Photo courtesy of the Portland Herald Press, Portland, Maine.*

Above: On February 19, 1964 the Coast Guard cutter *Coos Bay*, returning from winter patrol on ocean station "Bravo" off Labrador received an SOS from the British motorship *Ambassador*, with a crew of 35. The ship was sinking in the Atlantic, 370 miles south of her position. High seas had upset two liferafts on the 18th and 14 crewmen were lost. **Below:** The *Ambassador* took a line from the *Coos Bay* and a raft was sent over. Six swimmers from the cutter in survival gear assisted the remaining crew members to board the cutter. One man was drowned in the rescue operations. *Photos courtesy of the U.S. Coast Guard, Washington, D.C.*

THE AMBASSADOR

An epic rescue took place in the North Atlantic after an SOS by the British motorship *Ambassador* which was sinking six-hundred miles southeast of Halifax. Four merchant ships were nearby and answered the distress call. The Italian liner *Vulcania*, the French ship *Carrier*, the American ship *City of Aima* and the Norwegian ship *Fruen* all came to the aid of the stricken vessel. The Coast Guard Cutter *Coos Bay* was returning to her home port of Portland, Maine after five weeks on winter patrol on ocean station "Bravo" off Labrador. The cutter immediately diverted and arrived on scene on February 19, 1964. Fourteen crewmen of the *Ambassador* had been lost when two of the liferafts in which they had abandoned ship were upset in mountainous seas the day before.

The Norwegian freighter *Fruen* had rescued nine crewmen and there were twelve men still aboard the sinking freighter. A lifeline was shot by men on the cutter to the steeply listing ship. The hazardous rescue operation was carried out with six swimmers in rubber suits on the *Coos Bay* who dove in the water to assist the survivors after an attempt was made to use a large rubber raft. The towering waves capsized the raft. The Coastguardsmen managed to pull the remaining men from the sinking ship over another line to the cutter. It was fortunate that the ship was located that far out at sea as the rescue effort was carried out in the Gulf Stream where the water temperature was sixty-four degrees. They rescued eleven survivors over the rough seas. The twelfth man drowned while tied to a lifeline with three others as they were pulled across the span of lashing waves. The cutter returned with her eleven survivors to Portland, Maine on February 24, 1964.

In late January, 1964, the British supertanker *Federal Monarch* was crippled by a burned out main engine bearing, seventeen miles off Portland, Maine. The tug *Helen B. Moran* passed lines and then towed the huge tanker into Portland harbor for repairs. *Photo by Gardner Roberts, Portland Press Herald.*

Above: On March 1, 1964, the Liberian tanker *Amphialos* was battling a North Atlantic storm and heavy seas when the vessel broke in half. The bow section sank and the stern was taken in tow by the salvage tug *Curb* of the Merrit, Chapman and Scott Company of New York. The remaining section of the ship sank about 250 miles east of Boston. **Below:** On February 23, 1967 crewmen from the sinking fishing vessel *Maureen & Michael* were rescued by a rubber raft in the rough and cold North Atlantic. The raft was from the Coast Guard cutter *Castle Rock* which was on her way to the ocean station "Delta." She answered the vessel's SOS and saved the crew of eight and landed them at St. John's, Newfoundland. *Photos courtesy of the U.S. Coast Guard, Washington, D.C.*

Above: The 83′ sardine carrier *Mary Ann* was on her way from Rockland to Boothbay on October 24, 1965 when she ran up on Thrumcap Island in Johns Bay. The Captain, Elliott Wottom, was rescued by Coast Guardsmen from the Boothbay Harbor station. Salvage attempts on the fishing vessel failed and she was a total loss. *Photo courtesy of the Fisherman's Museum at Pemaquid Point, Maine.* **Below:** Two Maine couples drowned within 75 feet of shore off Monhegan Island on May 27, 1970. A thirty foot ketch ran aground on a ledge and sank in heavy seas and dense fog. The mainmast of the ketch *Thalassa* rose above the water in Lobster Cove on the southwest side of the island. The tragedy was not discovered until the fog lifted and the bodies were seen in the water by local fishermen. *Photo by Gardner Roberts, Portland Press Herald.*

The two masted schooner *Mattie* of Camden, ran aground on Bold Island, off Stonington on August 5, 1970. The vacationists aboard were removed by the schooner *Stephen Tabor*. The Coast Guard sent a boat to the scene but the schooner floated off at high tide with little damage. *Photo by Hammer, courtesy of the Courier Gazette, Rockland, Maine.*

Above: In July, 1972, the Norweigan tanker *Tamano* struck a buoy and ran up on a ledge near Hussey Shoal in Portland, Maine. The large tanker spilled 100,000 gallons of heavy petroleum into the waters of Portland Harbor and a containment boom was secured around the grounded vessel. **Below:** A few days later, still hard aground, the oil slick is contained in the boom as a small coastal tanker unloads the cargo from the *Tamano. Photos courtesy of Portland Press Herald.*

Above: The fishing vessel *Alton A*. and a Coast Guard 44-foot motor lifeboat were smashed onto the rocks at Cape Elizabeth, on December 5, 1972. The fishing boat had gone aground, and the Coast Guard boat went to the aid of the grounded vessel when seas became worse and both boats were in trouble. The crew of both were assisted ashore by hawsers, hand over hand through the waves with help from shore. **Below:** Efforts to save the boats were carried on through the night hours but were futile. *Photos courtesy of the Maine Histroical Society, Portland, Maine.*

Above: The *Alton A.* was a total loss but the Coast Guard 44-footer was lifted gently off the rocks by a crane the next day following the accident. **Below:** The Portland trawler *St. Patrick* ran onto rocks in thick fog at Ships' Cove on Cape Elizabeth, late in the afternoon of July 31, 1973. The Coast Guard sent a 40-foot patrol boat to assist the trawler. The boat heaved a line to the grounded vessel and maintained a constant pull on the trawler until she floated free about four hours later at high tide. None of the eight crewmen aboard was injured but rocks penetrated the hull and it had to be repaired. *Photo by Walter Elwell, courtesy of the Maine Historical Society, Portland, Maine.*

Saint Nicholas is the patron saint of mariners. On August 3, 1973 he was watching closely over the crew of a fishing vessel bearing his name when it was in collision with the ferry *Prince of Fundy*, twenty miles southwest of Matinicus Island. The seven man crew was shaken up but there were no injuries when the 387-foot ferry hit the bow of the fishing vessel in dense fog. The dragger was extensively damaged above the water line and was towed into Rockland by the Coast Guard cutter *Snohomish*. *Photo by Steven Lang, Owls Head, Maine.*

Above: The venerable steam tug *Seguin,* built in Bath in the winter of 1884, is the oldest vessel on the U.S. Register. Shown in her prime, the veteran tug spent her early years on the Kennebec towing schooners, attending launchings of the famous down-easters and making longer trips to Boston and New York. She finished her working days on Penobscot Bay. In 1969, she was donated to the Bath Marine Museum by Clyde B. Holmes, owner of the Eastern Towboat Company. **Below:** She was loaned to the Boothbay Schooner Museum in 1971 and in 1973 she sank at her dock. The tugboat is presently undergoing restoration at the Percy & Small shipyard at Bath. *Photos courtesy of the Bath Marine Museum.*

Above: On May 12, 1974 the Canadian freighter *Jennifer* was on her way from St. John, N.B., to New York City with a cargo of 1,300 tons of raw sugar. While off the coast of Maine the cargo shifted, resulting in a 14 degree list. The Coast Guard escorted the vessel into Bar Harbor and grounded her near the shore next to the Yarmouth ferry terminal. **Below:** The wet sticky sugar cargo was unloaded onto the Bar Harbor municipal pier from where it was trucked away. The *Jennifer* then left for repairs at a shipyard in East Boston. The ship was lost on December 2, 1974, when she sank in Lake Michigan during a gale, twenty miles northeast of Milwaukee, Wisconsin. The 15 crewmen were saved. *Photos by John Megas, Ellsworth American, Ellsworth, Maine.*

Above: The Cypriot tanker *Athenian Star* anchored off Portsmouth, New Hampshire in February 1975, after sustaining sea damage on a trip across the Atlantic. *Photo by Bill Van Valkenburg, U.S.C.G.* **Below:** The ship had underwater cracks in her hull as well as a waterline hole in her port bow where steel plates had been torn off in heavy seas. Her cargo was discharged into coastal tankers while at anchor and then she proceeded to Boston for repairs. *Photo by Richard Griggs, U.S.C.G.*

THE PENOBSCOT BAY SEA SERPENT

There are many stories about sea serpents. Perhaps the most famous is the Loch Ness Monster in Scotland called "Nessie." One has been reported in Penobscot Bay and might appropriately be called "Scotty." These apparitions have been rumored, but never proved to exist. Most publications list the phenomena as ficticious but many sea faring men have described sighting what appears to be an honest to goodness sea serpent. Many sailors hardly believe what they see at the time and nothing is revealed until later; say perhaps, that special night at the tavern when a few extra ounces of spirits tend to loosen a tongue. The serpent gets bigger with every drink. The stories are embellished in the re-telling until the thing is as big as a ship and twice as long.

The description of a sea serpent varies in proportion to the degree of inebriation. Sometimes six hundred feet in length, lying in the water in many folds or appearing like hogsheads floating in a line at a distance from each other. It has a head similar to that of a horse with glistening eyes, a mane of seaweed and nostrils that breathe smoke and fire. Have sea serpents been seen in Maine waters? The reports are mostly third or fourth hand, tending to border on hearsay. They are most always seen in Penobscot Bay in the fog and mist. Often, the serpent will rise up from the depths and cruise along in the fog. A logical explanation is offered by a scientist. A line of porpoises, leaping out of water would create the effect of many folds. The fire-breathing head is of course in the imagination of the one who sights the creature. Logical reasoning however, is not half as much fun as imaginative scuttlebutt.

This is an artist's conception of *"Scotty"* the Penobscot Bay Sea Serpent. In the early days, when serpents were seen off shore, often the result of demon rum, Maine was a dry state. Scientists have likened the sea serpent to a line of porpoises leaping out of water. *Drawing by Paul C. Morris, Nantucket, Massachusetts.*

During a southeast gale on the night of January 19, 1975 the lobster boat *Miss Fay III* broke from its mooring and grounded on the rocks at New Harbor and stove in her planking. The hull was a total loss but owner Norman Bookers salvaged the machinery and electronic gear. These parts were installed on a new boat named *Miss Faye IV*. Photo by Norman Davis, New Harbor, Maine.

SAILORS SUPERSTITIONS

There are many eerie tales of the sea and of shipwrecks. When disaster strikes, the surviving crewmen might blame the wreck on a violation of some old established tradition of the sea. There were many customs and legends born in the age of sail and have been continued down through the years. Many are still observed today. There are various taboos that sailors still believe. Never sail on Friday, never use blue paint and knock on wood to continue good fortune. It was an ill omen to see the phantom ship of the Flying Dutchman, a maritime legend about a Captain who cursed the sea gods and was condemned to roam the seas forever. Another popular one was red sky at night, sailors delight. Red sky in the morning, sailors take warning. This myth is more or less based on a keen weather eye. Violating some of these taboos may risk damage to yourself or your ship. Some sailors today depend on these traditions to relieve their anxieties. Obeying the customs gives the mariner peace of mine and a feeling of freedom from harm.

Most of the apprehension is from phenomena that are highly imaginative. The superstitions stem from ignorance and fear of the unknown. Tales passed down through the years tell of large sea creatures that attack ships or giant waves that can carry a vessel down to Davy Jones' Locker at the bottom of the sea. Violent storms that can smash a ship against huge rocks killing all on board. As the years passed, man's understanding of the sea grew and most of the phobias disappeared along with some superstitions, but not all. Some of the old customs are hard to lose and are still carried out today. They still break a bottle of champagne on the bow of a ship when she is launched—for good luck. The traditions of the sea add some fascinating nostalgia to the computer world of today.

The Japanese freighter *Musashino Maru* aground at Searsport, Maine, on February 2, 1976. There were heavy rains and high winds and visibility was limited. Her bottom was holed by the rocks. *Photo by Bob Beattie.*

THE MUSASHINO MARU

The modern cargo ships are equipped with all of the latest aids to navigation. They are not easily run aground, but high winds and adverse circumstances sometimes change the rules. The Japanese freighter *Musashino Maru* was grounded near Searsport during a severe coastal storm on February 2, 1976. The vessel arrived light and was blown ashore on Moose Point at 5:30 a.m. by hurricane force winds. The 362-foot refrigerator ship sprang a leak in a fuel tank resulting in 150 to 200 gallons of oil being spilled along the shore. The ship was to have loaded fifteen thousand tons of frozen french fried potatoes for shipment to the United Kingdom.

As she came ashore during an abnormally high tide, they had to wait for two weeks for another such tide before they could attempt to refloat her. In that time the ship became a major sight-seeing attraction. At time, there were one hundred automobiles parked along Route 1 in Searsport. People crossed over private property to see the grounded vessel and property owners along the shore had to hire security guards to prevent sightseers from trespassing on their land. On February 15th, the combined efforts of five tugs freed the freighter from the rocky shore and she was later towed to St. John, New Brunswick for drydocking and repairs.

On February 15th the tugs refloated the *Musashino Maru* in Penobscot Bay and then towed her to St. John, N.B. for repairs. *Aerial photo by John Laitin, Republican Journal, Belfast, Maine.*

Above: The coastal tanker *Vincent Tibbets* went aground on the rocks at Cow Island just outside Portland, Maine, on August 3, 1977. The vessel was carrying 2,900 barrels of oil at the time. She was pulled off the rocks the next day, without damage, by the tug *Celtic*. There was no oil spilled while the vessel was aground. *Photo courtesy of Guy Gannett Publications, Portland.* **Below:** Picked up just before they got their feet wet, two South Portland Lobstermen climb aboard a Coast Guard patrol boat after their boat went down on October 14, 1977 in Portland harbor. The low tide caused the vessel to ride onto an old submerged piling, roll over and sink. *Photo by Jim Daniels, courtesy of the Portland Press Herald.*

The 49-foot steel hulled fishing vessel *Northern Miner* went aground on Egg Rock in Frenchmen's Bay in August, 1981. The boat was pulled off on the next high tide with only minor damage. The grounding occurred at night. Egg Rock is the only island ledge with a light house (which was operating at the time) and there was no explanation given as to why the vessel grounded. *Photo by Earl Brechlin, Bar Harbor Times, Bar Harbor, Maine.*

CHAPTER TWELVE

The Portland Gale which occurred in November 1898, was described in Chapter three. The Life Saving Service Annual Report called it: "A cyclonic tempest, raging with unprecedented violence for 24 hours and with gradually abating force for twelve hours longer." The blizzard of February 7, 1978 was a similar type of storm with driving snow, high winds and high tides flooding coastal areas during the height of the storm. Except for Cape Cod, New England was paralyzed by the blizzard. The storm brought down power lines causing blackouts. Airports closed. Highways became clogged with heavy drifts and then motor vehicles that bogged down in the high drifts. States of Emergency were declared all over the northeast and thousands of persons were evacuated as high tides swept into low lying coastal areas. Helicopters were pressed into service following the storm to airlift patients to hospitals. The Federal Disaster Assistance Administration sent troops to the beleaguered New England states to help with snow removal and to rescue stranded motorists.

The storm inundated the southern Maine coast destroying many buildings and piers along the waterfronts. Three lighthouses were damaged by the high waves and the famous amusement pier at Old Orchard Beach was mostly demolished by the angry seas. In York County, tides of 16 to 18 feet, whipped by 40-50 m.p.h. winds were recorded in coastal areas during the storm. Most of the residents of the beach front were evacuated. National Guard Troops were dispatched by Governor James B. Longley to Cumberland and York counties to assist coastal communities. The Guardsmen brought heavy equipment and manpower to help shore up the waterfront area and to furnish security for the towns. The storm inflicted damage on shorefronts from Kittery to Bar Harbor. Most of the area shut down for a day to dig out as snow flurries continued into the next day. As the exhausted rescue crews and law enforcement personnel took a well deserved rest, the Maine ski areas reported the snowfall was well over three feet and skiing was fabulous.

159

On January 31, 1978 the Bouchard oil barge, B No. 105 was loading oil at the Atlantic Terminal dock in Newington, N.H. The stress sheared the hull and she broke in two pieces. About 7,000 gallons of oil were spilled into the Piscatacqua River above Portsmouth and had to be cleaned up. The barge was towed to New Jersey for repairs. *Wide World Photos.*

Above: Smuggling has once again become popular along the coast of Maine. In April 1978, a police raid resulted in the arrest of 31 persons. They had been unloading 70 pound bales of marijuana from the diesel yacht *Onalay* at a secluded cove at the mouth of the Damariscotta River in Boothbay. **Below:** The yacht was seized along with an estimated twenty tons of Marijuana. *Photos courtesy of the Boothbay Register, Boothbay Harbor, Maine.*

Above and Below: The two masted schooner *John F. Leavitt* on the ways on August 7, 1979 on the day before launching. Four years in the construction, the 100 ton vessel showed some handsome lines, her hull a well built piece of work by R.L. Wallace & Sons in Thomaston, Maine. *Steve Lang photos.*

On November 11, 1979, the *John F. Leavitt* departed her builders dock in Thomaston, Maine for a voyage to Quincy, Massachusetts to load her first cargo. The start of the voyage was perhaps symbolic of what was to happen later when she ran aground on a mussel bed in the St. George River. The maiden voyage was thus delayed for twelve hours until the incoming tide floated the schooner. The only damage suffered was perhaps to the ego of her skipper, Ned Ackerman. *Photo by Steven Lang, Owls Head.*

THE JOHN F. LEAVITT

The two masted schooner *John F. Leavitt* was launched on August 8, 1979, from the shipyard of R.L. Wallace in Thomaston, Maine. The vessel was built in an attempt to revive the coastal schooner as an inexpensive freighter carrier. The schooner left Thomaston in November 1979, and immediately ran aground on a mussel bed in the St. George River, a short way from her dock. She floated off on the tide and sailed to Quincy, Massachusetts to load cargo. The 78 ton mixed cargo was taken aboard and the vessel left Quincy on December 20th bound for Haiti. The schooner ran into a storm after a short while in the North Atlantic and on December 27th, sent a radio call for help. Helicopters removed the crew and the vessel was not seen again and was presumed lost. The primary cause for the loss of the *John F. Leavitt* was attributed to the inexperience of her Captain and crew.

A dangerous coastal storm on October 25-26, 1980 swept up the coast of Maine wreaking havoc in the harbors along the way. The winds were clocked at 65 knots and the fifty foot trawler *Walborg* was wrecked on the rocks at Sherman's Cove in Camden after her mooring lines parted. *Photo by P.J. Hamel, Camden, Maine.*

Above: The October 1980 storm wrecked numerous fishing boats along the coast of Maine. The gale winds caused a 36′ lobsterboat to break away from her mooring and then to smash into pieces on Lincolnville Beach. The vessel belonged to Lincolnville's harbormaster Richard Stearns and was a total wreck. *Photo by Tom Von Malder, Courier-Gazette, Rockland.* **Below:** The oil tanker *Christian F. Reinauer* struck an underwater ledge about two miles northwest of Metinic Island in West Penoboscot Bay on November 21, 1980. The Boston tanker had an eight foot underwater gash in her hull and leaked an estimated 80,000 gallons of home heating oil and gasoline into Penobscot Bay. A large tanker barge was brought in and removed the remaining cargo from the small tanker and later she steamed to a New York drydock for repairs. *Wide World Photo.*

The presentation of Silver Lifesaving Medals to Steven Rollins on the left, and Sherman Stanley by Capt. William J. Brogdon, Jr., commander of the Coast Guard Group Portland who said: "they displayed remarkable seamanship, endurance and daring and that their courageous and unselfish actions uphold the highest traditions of the sea." *Photo by Tom Davis, courtesy of Down East Magazine.*

TWO SILVER MEDALS

"IN TESTIMONY OF HEROIC DEEDS IN SAVING LIFE FROM THE PERILS OF THE SEA." These words encircle the silver lifesaving medals which were presented by the U.S. Coast Guard to Sherman M. Stanley, Sr., and Steven Rollins of Monhegan Island for their daring rescue of two stranded Coastguardsmen from Smuttynose Rock on February 2, 1981 in gale winds and high seas. Their citation reads: "For heroic action on the morning of 2 February 1981 when they rescued two Coastguardsmen from Smuttynose Rock, Maine. At about midnight, during a severe storm, the light on Monhegan Island lost power and two Coastguardsmen launched their 16 foot outboard motorboat from Manana Island to tend the light. While attempting to cover the distance between the islands, the engine failed. Driven by high winds, the boat was blown onto Smuttynose Rock between Manana and Monhegan Islands and capsized. The two Coastguardsmen scrambled onto the rocks and immediately called for help on their portable radio. A motor lifeboat and a helicopter were dispatched with an estimated time of arrival of several hours. Meanwhile the stranded men, huddled on the rocks, exposed to the wind and spray, were suffering from hypothermia. The Officer-in-charge of Coast Guard Station Boothbay Harbor called Mr. Stanley, a Monhegan Harbor pilot, and asked if he could help. Mr. Stanley called Steven Rollins, the Harbor Master of Monhegan and advised him of the request. The men quickly launched a 16-foot dory and, despite heavy seas, darkness and 40 knot winds, began to row the dory over 300 yards to Smuttynose Rock. Reaching the scene they found it impossible to approach the rocks because of the breaking seas. Undaunted, they left the relative security of the harbor and rowed around the island to reach the lee side of Smuttynose. Displaying remarkable seamanship, they backed the dory into the rocks and the stranded men jumped aboard. They then rowed the overloaded dory into the teeth of the storm to safety at Monhegan Island. The determined efforts of Mr. Stanley and Mr. Rollins and the outstanding initiative and fortitude during this rescue were instrumental in the saving of the two men's lives. Their unselfish actions and valiant service reflect great credit upon themselves and are in keeping with the highest traditions of humanitarian service." The citation was signed by the Commandant of the U.S. Coast Guard, Admiral J.B. Hayes, October 29, 1981 in Washington, D.C. "...Greater love hath no man than to lay down his life for his brother."

Above: On July 8, 1981 the Tancook Whaler *Vernon Langille* struck the Carlton Bridge in Bath. A strong current and a dying wind pulled the vessel off course and her masts struck the fixed span of the bridge tipping her over on her beam ends. Small craft in the area picked up the crew and brought them ashore. A tug from the Bath Iron Works hooked on to the sailing vessel and towed the submerged schooner to the Iron Works dock where she was refloated. There were no injuries to the crew. In a couple of weeks the vessel was refitted and back sailing again on the Kennebec. *Photo courtesy of a friend.* **Below:** A posh eighty-foot yacht was wrecked in Cushing Harbor on August 24, 1981. The *Bull Moose* went aground on a ledge off Flea Island during a wind squall. The boat settled bow down in the mud when the tide went out and she filled with water when the tide came in. The yacht, valued at approximately two million dollars, was owned in Baltimore, Maryland. The vessel was salvaged by a crane on a barge. The hull was still sound but the luxurious interior of the boat was ruined. *Photo by Terry Dodge, courtesy of the Rockland Courier-Gazette.*

Above: Bruised egos are commonplace among yachting skippers in Maine's narrow channels. On July 25, 1981, the 58-foot yacht *Ortem* ran aground on Basin Point in South Harpswell at about 7:30 a.m. The vessel hit the submerged ledge on a falling tide. There was little damage and the yacht floated free in the afternoon on the high tide. *Photo by Don Hickley, Brunswick.* **Below:** Waiting for the tide to come in is like watching and waiting for water to boil. On September 16, 1982, Albert Payson of South Portland ran up on some rocks at Willard Beach on the outgoing tide and had a long wait for the tide to refloat him. *Photo courtesy of Portland Press Herald.*

At the pier in Boothbay Harbor, State Police unloaded an estimated 25-30 tons of marijuana from the Columbian freighter *Indomable* on November 15, 1982. The weed was reported to have been worth about fifteen million dollars. Twenty-four men were arrested in a police raid at Bremen early in the morning. *Photo by Robert Lucas, courtesy of the Rockland Courier-Gazette.*

SMUGGLING IN MAINE

Webster's dictionary defines smuggling as: "importing or exporting secretly, without paying duties, or to convey clandestinely." In the days before the Revolutionary War, smuggling was patriotic to beat the taxes imposed by England. There was not much contraband in the 19th century until the "Maine Law" went into effect in 1851. After that, liquor was smuggled into Maine on a regular basis. The roaring 20's arrived with Prohibition and soon there wasn't any room in the lobster pots off shore for the lobsters, they were full of whiskey bottles. Illegal liquor came to Maine in large quantities during Prohibition because it was so easy to bring ashore. The Maine fishermen knew their waters quite well. The secluded coves with hidden underwater ledges were areas where law enforcement officials could not navigate, and the smugglers profited. Prohibition was an unpopular law that made the gangster rich. Today the drug smugglers have turned to the Maine coast as a landing place for their illegal cargoes.

In 1981, a Federal crackdown on drug smugglers in Florida drove them north. Officials felt that Maine was becoming a distribution center for the illicit cargoes. With the Coast Guard vessels in need of repairs, the budget cuts in Washington aided the smugglers, but there were some successful results. Drug arrests in Maine have grown in the past few years. In May of 1977, one and one half tons of marijuana was seized. In 1978, another twenty tons was seized and in 1980, thirty-four tons was apprehended at Stonington. In November 1982, thirty tons of the illegal weed was taken along with twenty-four men, ten of them from Maine. The Columbian freighter *Indomable* had landed at a Bremen lobster pier early in the evening of November 13th, only to be met by law enforcement officials and then arrested. The Coast Guard brought the boat to Boothbay Harbor where the contraband was unloaded by State Police and trucked away.

Above: The remains of the full rigged ship *St. Mary,* built in Phippsburg in 1890. The vessel was in a collision with another ship while rounding Cape Horn in August of 1890. While returning to the Falkland Islands she ran aground and became a total wreck. *Photo by Nicholas Dean, North Edgecomb, Maine.* **Below:** The beams, the knees and part of the planking of the *St. Mary* are on exhibit at the Maine State Museum at Augusta. *Photo by William P. Quinn.*

A set of commemorative stamps issued in the Falkland Islands just prior to the 1982 war between Argentina and Great Britain shows five shipwrecks scattered around the Islands. Two of these are Maine-built vessels. Most Falklands issues are coveted by philatelists because of their scarcity. The 25p stamp has the remains of the *Snow Squall,* a small clipper built in South Portland in 1851. The 26p stamp depicts the *St. Mary* wreck, a full rigged ship built in Phippsburg in 1890 and wrecked on her maiden voyage around Cape Horn.

THE ST. MARY

The skeletons of numerous Maine ships lie among the ghost fleet of the Falklands. The hulks and wrecks, more than 200 vessels, including clippers and down-easters dot the local shores and resemble a graveyard of ships. Sailing vessels were disabled trying to go around Cape Horn at the tip of South America. One of these, the *St. Mary,* was launched in Phippsburg in 1890 and tragically, less than five months later, lay cast ashore at Kelp Lagoon, thirty miles south of Port Stanley. In 1978, an expedition to the Falkland Islands by the National Maritime Historical Society was responsible for a vast project; to bring back a 25 ton, 40-foot starboard section of the *St. Mary.* The section was cut with chain saws into forty pieces and transported to the Maine State Museum at Augusta, next door to the State House. The jigsaw puzzle was re-assembled and the exhibit opened in the summer of 1980. Museum visitors can walk on deck now and sense the aura of a wooden square rigged ship.

The rotting hull of the Maine clipper ship *Snow Squall* lies in Stanley Harbor in the Falkland Islands. Built in 1851, the Maine clipper was wrecked in 1864. *Photo by Nicholas Dean, No. Edgecomb, Maine.*

The pictures and stories throughout this book have depicted ships and boats in their final days. An interesting contrast is presented in photographs taken in the spring of 1982 on Beals Island. New ideas and innovations are labor savers and are inclined to make life easier for all. But sometimes, the old fashion ways are better. Calvin Beal, Jr., moved his new lobster boat, the *Rachael Ann* from the boat shop to the water in the traditional manner. He assembled about twenty volunteers, his friends and neighbors, to act as a human cradle for the new boat while it was moved on rollers and pulled over the road by a truck. When they arrived at the launch site where the truck could not maneuver, the men took over and muscled the boat into the water. The most important factor was teamwork. The result proved conclusive. *Photographs by Brenda T. Dodge, Beals, Maine.*

The dragger *John Neptune* went aground at Spruce Point near Boothbay Harbor early in the morning of December 7, 1982. Coast Guard reports on the incident stated that the Captain had gone below for a moment and had left the vessel on auto-pilot when she grounded. The fishing vessel out of Portland had a fare of fish aboard and was bound for the harbor to sell the load. On the afternoon tide, the boat floated off the rocks with little damage. *Photo by Emily Lee Berne, courtesy of the Boothbay Register, Boothbay Harbor, Maine.*

Fishing is a fifty million dollar industry in Maine. The state is famous for her lobster fishery, but clams, ocean food fish and sardines are an important part of the catch also. Maine fishermen have a dangerous occupation when the weather turns bad. In February 1982, the 40-foot gillnetter *Chica,* out of Portland sent a "may-day" to the Coast Guard. Within one hour of the call, Coast Guard units were on the scene thirty miles southeast of Portland searching for the boat. Two dozen fishermen from the Portland area joined in the hunt and for three days they searched in cold winds, rain and fog along with aircraft from the Coast Guard and Navy and other Coast Guard boats. The search covered 6,800 square miles of ocean but all they found was debris and a hatch cover. The boat and crew were never found.

About 11 a.m. on December 12, 1982, the 124-foot steel fishing vessel *Robert Powell* began taking on water in the Gulf of Maine. A leak was discovered in the engine room. Conditions worsened and Captain James Dow radioed the Coast Guard for help but helicopters at the Cape Cod Air Station could not fly because of icing conditions. The wind was gusting to 50 miles per hour in driving snow with only ¼ mile visibility. At 3 p.m. the five men abandoned ship and went into a 4' x 8' life raft. Soon the raft began to leak and the men found themselves in water up to their waists. They kept bailing but the water was gaining on them. In the meantime, the Coast Guard had directed another fishing vessel, the *Kathleen & Julie II* to the scene. Her Captain spotted a flare that had been fired from the life raft. The men on the raft were hauled aboard the *Kathleen & Julie II* just in time. They had turned blue from the cold and couldn't have held on much longer. On Monday December 13th, the fishing vessel returned the survivors to their families in Portland.

Above: The Bath Iron Works on the Kennebec River. Since the early 1700's ships have slid down the ways into the river. Today, ocean going vessels of all types are constructed in Bath carrying on the traditions of 300 years of American Shipbuilding. *Aerial Photo by William P. Quinn.*
Below: In August 1981, Bar Harbor received a royal visitor. The Cunard Liner Queen Elizabeth II made her first trip to the noted resort town. The ship moored just offshore of the town. *Photo by Earl Brechlin; Bar Harbor Times, Bar Harbor, Maine.*

Above: The motor vessel *Bluenose* ran from Bar Harbor to Yarmouth, Nova Scotia for twenty-six years, was taken out of service in mid-October, 1982. The ferry was moored at Yarmouth and put up for sale. A new larger, more modern vessel replaced the old one and was also named *Bluenose. Photo courtesy of Canadian National Marine.* **Below:** Daily summer service between Portland and Yarmouth, N.S. is via the luxury cruise ferry *Scotia Prince.* The 411-foot vessel carries 1500 passengers and 250 vehicles. Her enclosed decks contain dining rooms, cocktail bars, lounges, casinos, duty free shops and accommodations for 800. Built in Europe in 1972, the *Scotia Prince* was operated between Sweden and Germany before she was brought to Maine. *Aerial Photo by William P. Quinn.*

On December 16, 1982, a 130-foot barge with a 50 ton crane aboard was torn from its mooring off Prouts Neck in Scarborough and smashed onto the rocks during a storm. No one was on board at the time. The barge and crane were being used to lay an underwater pipe as part of an ocean outfall sewer project. *Photo by William P. Quinn.*

The 130-foot barge hit a prominent headland and sixty mile an hour winds and 17-foot seas pounded the steel barge into pieces and lay it on the rocks. Value of the equipment lost was listed as $60,000. *Aerial Photo by William P. Quinn, Plane piloted by Hank Dempsey.*

In the past century, many ships have laid their bones on the rocky coast of Maine. In the early days, the sailing ship wrecks were frequent. When steam power came, the number of accidents was reduced somewhat but man still made mistakes. The iron hulled vessels were bigger than the sailing ships, but the only contrast was a larger wreck. Today, the wrecks are less frequent but nevertheless do still occur. The storms still rage and the oceans claim victims as before but in an automated age, with space age navigation, the results are not always as tragic in lives lost.

Modern satellite weather forecasting aids the mariner and gives him a few days warning of the approach of killer storms. The development of modern ships has helped to reduce mishaps on the high seas and along the shore. The design, power and reliability of these ships result in fewer accidents. The latest navigational devices help mariners pin-point their location at sea using satellites locked into orbit around the earth. The beautiful sailing vessels are no longer engaged in world commerce. Theirs was a fascinating era that is witnessed today only on special occasions. The steam and diesel powered ships dominate the oceans today.

The End

ACKNOWLEDGEMENTS

The collection of photographs in this book required an extensive search all along the coast of Maine. Some pictures were borrowed and copied while others were purchased. Many thanks to all who have supplied the photographs, information and encouragement. There are many friends who have contributed much and a special "Thank You" goes to: Roger Peterson, Gardner Roberts, Frank Claes, Steven Lang, Jim Stevens, Captain W.J.L. Parker, U.S.C.G. (Ret.), David Crockett, Marnee Small, Susan Jones, Bob Beattie, Betty Beattie, Clara Burton, Laura Brown, Brewster Harding, Jane Stevens, Captain Rodney Ross III, Jamie Stahl, John Lochhead, Sandy Armentrout, Mr. & Mrs. Russell Bryant, J. Malcolm Barter, Arthur Fournier, Nicholas Dean, Paul Sherman, Mary Brewer, Ruth Watson, Mary Norton Orrick, Davis Thomas, Richard M. Boonisar, Dale Kuhnert, Gladys O'Neil, Richard Griggs, Hank Dempsey, Allie Ryan, Bob and Judy Mansfield, Christie Snow, Farnham W. Smith, John Megas, Bill Carter, John Fish and John Ullman. There were many others including Paul C. Morris of Nantucket who did the beautiful art work for the book. Deep gratitude to all those who helped me in the acquisition and assembly of this material.

W.P.Q.

CAMDEN HARBOR

BIBLIOGRAPHY

American Sailing Coasters of the North Atlantic,
  Paul C. Morris

Assignment in Military Intelligence, Harold W. Coffin

*A Maritime History of Bath, Maine and the Kennebec
  River Region,* William Avery Baker

Four Masted Schooners of the East Coast,
  Paul C. Morris

Islands of Maine, Bill Caldwell

Maine Almanac, Min Brunelle

Marine Salvage, Joseph N. Gores

Mt. Desert Island & Acadia National Park,
  Sargent F. Collier

Rum War at Sea, Malcolm R. Willoughby, U.S.C.G.

Steamboat Lore of the Penobscot, John M. Richardson

Storms and Shipwrecks of New England,
  Edward Rowe Snow

200 Years of Lubec History, Ryerson Johnson—Editor

The Coast of Maine, Louise Dickinson Rich

The Down Easters, Basil Lubbock

The Great Coal Schooners of New England,
  Capt. W.J.L. Parker, U.S.C.G. (Ret.)

The Last Sail Down East, Giles M.S. Tod

The Maine Islands, Dorothy Simpson

The Maritime History of Maine,
  William Hutchinson Rowe

Tidewater Ice of the Kennebec River, Jennie G. Everson

Up in Maine, Stories of Yankee Life Told in Verse,
  Holman F. Day

Wake of the Coasters, John F. Leavitt

GOVERNMENT PUBLICATIONS:

U.S. Coast Guard, Annual Reports: 1915 to 1921

U.S. Coast Pilot - Atlantic Coast (1) Eastport to
  Cape Cod

U.S. Life Saving Service, Annual Reports: 1876 to 1914

U.S. List of Merchant Vessels, Annual List: 1884 to
  1940

U.S. Revenue Cutter Service, Annual Reports: 1914 &
  1897

U.S. Department of Commerce survey charts: 13278,
  13286, 13288, 13290, 13302, 13312 & 13325

PERIODICALS:

Down East Magazine, Various issues through 1982

Steamboat Bill, Various issues through 1982

The Long Reach Log, Bath Marine Museum

The New York Maritime Register

Tow Line, Moran Towing Co., New York, N.Y.

NEWSPAPERS:

The Bangor Daily Commercial

The Bangor Daily News

The Bar Harbor Times

The Bath Daily News

The Boothbay Register

The Boston Globe

The Courrier Gazette, Rockland

The Eastern Argus, Portland

The Evening Times Globe,
  St. John, New Brunswick, Canada

The National Fisherman, Camden

The New York Times

The Portland Press Herald

The Republican Journal, Belfast

The Telegraph Journal, St. John, New Brunswick

The Times Record, Brunswick

MUSEUMS:

Bath Marine Museum, Bath, Maine

Brickstore Museum, Kennebunk, Maine

Fisherman's Museum, Pemaquid Point

Kittery Marine Museum, Kittery, Maine

Maine State Museum, Augusta, Maine

Mariners Museum, Newport News, Virginia

Peabody Museum of Salem, Salem, Massachusetts

Penobscot Marine Museum, Searsport, Maine

HISTORICAL SOCIETIES:

Bar Harbor Historical Society

Border Historical Society, Eastport, Maine

Kennebunkport Historical Society

Maine Historical Society, Portland, Maine

Above: The *Reine Marie Stewart* was built in Thomaston in 1919 as a four masted barkentine of 1,307 tons and was 218 feet long. She entered the coal trade and sailed for a few years but her unpopular square rig laid her up prematurely. She remained at the dock in Thomaston for years and was the subject of artists and photographers. The above scene is taken from a post card circa 1920. In 1937, she was sold to Canadian interests and overhauled. She was re-rigged as a four masted schooner and sailed into the 1940's. In the summer of 1942, she was caught by a German submarine off the coast of Africa. Her crew left in the small boat and the sub sank the schooner with shell fire. **Below:** An interesting comparison can be made from the photo above and one taken in 1982. It reveals little change in the landscape at Thomaston. *Photo by William P. Quinn.*

181

Constructing a wooden schooner hull in an early Maine shipyard. *Drawing by Paul C. Morris, Nantucket, Massachusetts.*

A view taken aboard the wrecking lighter *Addie* preparing to refloat a schooner aground. The workmen are hoisting a 9,500 pound anchor to make it ready for setting. The big rope in the foreground is an 18″ hawser used with the beach gear. The beach gear is a rig consisting of anchors, buoys, hawsers and tackle used to haul stranded vessels afloat off sand bars, ledges and shorelines. Wrecking barges are equipped with booms, a hoisting engine and pumps and have a shallow draft, to get in close for work on the reefs. *Photo courtesy of Robert Beattie, Belfast, Maine.*